PARHAM DONYAI

HOW TO START A PROFITABLE BUSINESS

WITH NO PRIOR KNOWLEDGE
AND WITHOUT RISKING
YOUR MONEY

Parham Donyai

HOW TO START A PROFITABLE BUSINESS WITH NO PRIOR KNOWLEDGE AND WITHOUT RISKING YOUR MONEY

Parham Donyai LL.B(Hons),

Dip. Legal Practice,

MCSR, ITEC

Design: Vilius Musinskas

Published by: Active Press

ISBN: 978-1-5136-3926-0

For more information
please visit:
www.parhamdonyai.com

You live in a great age where there is an abundance of mentors, gurus, life coaches, business advisers and motivators everywhere. On any social media platform or on YouTube you can easily access lots of people who are great at business and can give you advice on how to start a business and how to be profitable. But can they? How do you know that the person proclaiming to be a master of business, really is good and is not just scamming you to take your money? How do you know they actually know how to start a business, run a business, deal with staff, hire and fire, pay people on time, negotiate, ask for credit if need be, take out insurance, keep track of their books and do a thousand other things needed to run a business? Most important of all, do they know how to run a "profitable" business?

You should always be very careful with your money and your time and the first step you need to take if you want to be successful and have a profitable business is to have the skill to not part with money unnecessarily, whether it is on a course or on a book or a seminar with someone that may not give you what you need. You don't need to be scared, you just need to be careful and ensure that you get something worth much more than what you put in, in terms of time and money. So, lesson number 1 is to be careful with your money and try and save as much as you can; never spend unless you have done your research and can justify that spend.

I've done the graft from a very early age and had several businesses which have been profitable and which I have grown from the bottom up. Yes, I have run actual brick and mortar as well as online businesses and dealt with all aspects of running an actual business. Over 20 years of business experience and many successes and a few failures have taught me a huge amount about business, marketing, advertising, branding, profit and loss. I am not counting businesses I ran when I was much younger, such as when I was buying and selling cars in my late teens.

In my book How to be a Successful Entrepreneur, I covered the basics of starting a business and answered many of the questions that I constantly get asked on social media about business and how to become successful. In this book I would like to address a more comprehensive question and tackle something that many many advisers don't really pay attention to and that is "profit".

You see, a business without profit is no business at all. Starting a business and generating money is not that difficult but overseeing the whole thing from the most minute details all the way to being profitable is another game. In my 20+ years of business I've had a lot of people work for me. Some gone on and started their own businesses and I can tell you the majority of them have failed. The reason why they failed is because they only dealt with one aspect of my business when they worked for me and never really understood the whole picture and how to put all the little pieces together to end up having a profitable business.

Why do you think so many businesses start but fail? Around 20% of small businesses fail in their first year, 30% of small business fail in their second year and 50% of small businesses fail after five years in business. These are rough statistics and very much industry and geography related. In fact, in some areas 90% of businesses fail within 5 years, many times much sooner.

Sometimes it's because of low turnover but often it's because they are just not profitable and it is profit that ensures long-term sustainability. This book is going to teach you how to be profitable and hopefully put some fundamental principles in place for you, so you remain profitable for the remainder of your business life.

Don't worry too much about having a big business or lots of employees or winning awards or expanding at the outset. The most important thing you need to worry about is to be profitable and unfortunately many business people forget this extremely important rule as their business gets bigger and things change, such as costs getting higher. No matter who you are or what business you have and how successful you've been, if you are not profitable, you will go out of business. If you've been lucky and you've saved up money during your business life, then that is very good but if you haven't saved up money and you don't have anything to fall back on, then not being profitable means the end of your business.

I haven't been to business school so I really don't know what they teach you in business school but I can tell you that many of the people that come out of business school, either don't start businesses or start businesses that end up failing. So, going to business school does not necessarily guarantee that you will have a successful business.

AN IMPORTANT EXAMPLE YOU SHOULD MAKE A NOTE OF AND REMEMBER

Imagine getting on a bicycle, starting to pedal and being stable as you ride it and then you start pedalling even harder to go even faster and you're not paying attention to the slight leaning on the side as you ride. You're concentrating way too much on going faster and what will happen eventually is that you will fall off the bike. You can try again or the fall may be so bad that you will get injured or your bike will be broken and you will no longer get the opportunity to ride that bike again - or any bike.

Keeping your balance on the bike is my analogy for being profitable. You should always worry about keeping your balance and not worry too much about going fast. As long as you're keeping your balance, you can start going a little bit faster but not at the expense of losing your balance. If you are not going fast enough to keep a balance, then in my analogy, you are not profitable and potentially making a loss.

This book is all about how you can keep your balance and I will remind you constantly that keeping your balance on the bike is the most important part of your business life. Going fast is wonderful but never at the expense of losing your balance; remember that.

This book is for you if you want to start a business or if you are already in business. If you're going to start a business, then this book will be extremely valuable to you. If you are already in business then this book will help you a lot in becoming profitable, staying profitable and hopefully making even more profit. If you are in business and things are very very bad and you have gone beyond the point of salvage, then this book may very well also help you in tidying things up and ensuring that you don't lose everything.

If you want to be successful, you need to start making some changes. That's assuming that you haven't been very successful up to this point or maybe you have plateaued. There are definitely things you can do to make sure you reach that success level you aspire to. Things you can change about yourself, people you can emulate and principles you can start implementing.

It's not always easy and it may not be overnight but millions of people become successful and wealthy, so there is no reason why it can't be you. If you are serious and tired of thinking about it, talking about it, dreaming about it and actually now want to do something about it, then let's get you started.

I don't know all the answers and I am not the most successful person in the world but I am more successful than over 99% of others. So, if you want to join the top 1%, then there are lots of things for you in the following pages that can be of use. I've said it before and will repeat it again here, what I will tell you are real life "practical" ways that you can become successful. I am not about all this baloney "think big" "have a dream" stuff without giving you actual ways to become successful.

Most business mentors and gurus have another motive which is to sell you more of their stuff. Right now, in writing my books, that is not my purpose or aim. You don't have to worry that I am giving you no real substance and leading you to buy a course or something. I am not. This one book is designed to help you start a profitable business in whatever field or whatever country. Anyone can do it.

WHAT IS SUCCESS?

Success is an extremely subjective thing. Some people class getting a job as becoming successful, some see exceeding in that job as success and others see becoming a billionaire as becoming successful.

Success is whatever "you" class as being success. Everyone has their own goals and standards and it is up to you to set your own goal and definition of success. One person's success is another person's failure. And discussing success can be a little bit like discussing religion!

As far as we are concerned for the purposes of this book, you must never let other people's success put you off yours or become a source of stress for you. In other words, you must never get frustrated by seeing other people succeed. If this is you, then this is the first thing you must address if you want to truly become successful.

You know the type. You see someone driving a Ferrari and instead of thinking wow, how did they do it, you call them names and wish they die!!! If this is you, get over it! You need to be nice to successful people, because they can teach you stuff! You also need to never have negative feelings when you see successful people. Positivity is the only route to success.

Other people's success must always be a source of inspiration and emulation for you. You must never see it as a negative thing. I say this because many people start comparing themselves with others and getting frustrated that they are are not doing as well as x or y person. Who knows? And who cares? The other person may have had a head-start, been lucky, done something illegal, been given some money, been at the right place at the right time, had more luck, done something different to what they say they have etc etc You will not know and it shouldn't bother you either. You are on your own journey and you may even be more successful in your own way. I am sure you will succeed, if you truly apply yourself.

TASK

The first task for you is to define your own success. So please grab a piece or paper and a pen and write down at the top of the page, what your ultimate definition of success is. For example, this can be "own a £100m mansion" or "make £1m" or "have a franchise business". Please go and write it down and come back.

Oh, so you are back? What did you write down? Look at it carefully. Does it have a monetary amount in there? Or is it something random like my 3rd example above? Did you write, "I want to make £100m" or did you write "I want to own my own yacht".

LET'S START WORKING ON YOUR MIND

The first thing you need to start working on is "figures". You need to start thinking in numbers. If you are not or have not been a numbers guy/gal until now, then this is the time to change it. You cannot have a profitable business if you don't think in numbers. The very definition of profit is totally intertwined with numbers.

Most importantly, to become successful, you need to not only understand numbers but be able to work with them and pay close attention to them. I tell you this as someone who has operated very successful real businesses and not someone who has just studied courses. Don't worry if you are bad at maths. I was terrible at maths (amongst other subjects!). I am not saying you need to become a maths guru. What I am saying is that whatever your ultimate definition of success in terms of business is going to be, it needs to have some numbers attached to it, otherwise you won't know where you are supposed to go, how long it will take you or how to adjust along the journey.

For example if your definition of success is to own a yacht, then please tell me how you are going to get there and how long it will take you? This is a very unspecific goal. What yacht? How big? How much will it cost? Where will it be moored? What will you do with it? How are you going to get it?

You see where I am going with this? Now let's change this example to a more practical one:

I want to own a 100 foot yacht made by Pershing in 10 years' time. The price of it will be $10m and I will dock it in Puerto Banus harbour. I will use it to hold business meetings. Or even better, I will rent it out weekly. By renting it out weekly, I will earn between $50-$100k. The cost of mooring it will be $100k per annum.

Or a more simple goal: I will be worth $50m in 10 years' time. The logistics of how you will do this will hopefully be worked out by you, by the time you finish reading this book!

The point I am trying to make is that if you are planning on becoming financially successful, you need to start thinking in numbers and associating everything with a number and a figure. Ideas are great and you must have big ideas for sure but you need to try and attach numbers to things.

Understandably at the outset, it may not be easy to attach numbers to ideas. This is why research and a business plan are so important. It is during this process that you find out how you are going to achieve your ultimate goal and more importantly, whether it is a viable route to take.

I was speaking to a group of people recently about the inventor John Taylor OBE who was also an entrepreneur. He always insisted that if he couldn't work something in his head from concept to successful conclusion, then he would not go ahead with it, however good the idea was.

This is such great advice. Successful people define what their definition of success is, as an overall thing and/or as small steps and work it out to a conclusion in terms of numbers and practicality and then if it all makes sense, they go ahead with it.

The purpose of this book is to help you with those initial ideas, get you to choose a workable worthy goal and show you the practical steps you need to take to get to your goal without losing hope or giving up. It can be done and you can do it. You just need to want it bad enough, which leads us to Mindset.

MINDSET

Getting the right mind-set is THE most important part of your journey to start a business and make it a profitable business. In fact, this section should really be its own book and as you know, there are countless books on getting the right mind-set for success. The mind is the initiator, the transporter and the concluder of all successful business ventures. Even more, the mind is the reason why you succeed and why you fail - in everything!

I was recently working with a young man who was being bullied at school and this lad was much bigger and stronger than the bully. He could punch the hell out of the bully, if he wanted to. He was more muscular, bigger and had been doing karate since he was 3! Why was he so afraid of the bully and just couldn't fight back? He was petrified of the bully!

The answer is of course, the mind. His mind was weaker in some way and something had happened to either him by himself or between the two of them that had meant despite his huge physical advantage, his mind lacked the relevant power to give him the success he needed over the bully.

I cannot emphasise enough how important the power of your mind is to your end success. Quite frankly, IT IS EVERYTHING. You must at the outset of any endeavour, get your mindset right. Once you have it truly in the right place, nothing should stop you from getting what you want.

A lot of the times you hear about this "mindset stuff" and you may or may not truly understand what is meant by it. Do you? In order for you to be in the right place to become successful, you need to now start looking back at what has been effective for you in your life. You need to start looking at your own mindset. I say this because there are 2 types of people out there:

1. People who see others' success and can understand and interpret how "they" did something and then go about and emulate it.

2. People who, no matter how many success biographies they read, cannot put "themselves" in the shoes of the successful person. If this is you, then you need to start by looking at your own successes, however small or large.

TASK

You need to take some time now, go and sit in a quiet room with a pen and paper and write down the top 10 most successful things you have achieved in your life so far. It can be anything from making X amount of money from that garage sale when you were 14 or getting it on with that girl you fancied when you were 22 to getting a yes from your 3rd interview at a big firm. Write a top 10 list and come back.

OK, so you're back? Did you do it properly as asked? How far are your number 1 to number 10 in terms of effort? What were the things that numbers 1-10 had in common? This is such an IMPORTANT exercise for you to do.

TASK

Write down the 5-10 common things shared between numbers 1-10. It doesn't have to be "mind" things; just things that are common.

For example:

Getting together with Amanda

1. I really liked her 2. I didn't listen to my mum 3. I really wanted her 4. I had to exaggerate who I was. 5. I didn't see my friends or go out with them for ages. 6. I saved up all my money to take her out. etc etc

Buying my first bike

1. I really wanted it 2. I saved up loads 3. I didn't go drinking after I got it any more and became healthier 4. My dad said it was a waste and I wouldn't ride it 5. I planned for it. etc etc

If you were to do this exercise for all 10 things, you will start finding common denominators. They will be specific to you and can be things like:

1. I really wanted it.
2. I didn't care about anything but that.

3. I felt ashamed not having/having it.

4. I gave up everything to have it.

5. I didn't listen to others.

Now, using the same 10 examples of success, write down 10 things you felt/saw/smelt at the time when you succeeded in your endeavour. These can be things like:

1. I felt on top of the world.

2. I was crying with joy.

3. We finished in Nantes and I could smell the fresh flowers everywhere.

4. Everyone was praising me and telling me how great I had done.

5. The feeling of her touch on my skin was amazing.

etc etc.

In order for you to put in place the right mental foundation for success in your chosen endeavour, you need to ideally emulate other successful people and what they did/do to achieve success but more importantly, you need to access your own databank of success and emulate the steps.

Following on from the above exercises you need to decipher what it is that gets "you" going. What are the important things to you. What turns you on to start something and not give up AND to take it to a final conclusion. Tap into the feelings, smells, triggers, anchors and sounds of prior successes and bring them into play.

For example, what gets me going is all the previous experiences I have had in life. Driving around Europe, staying in amazing places, travelling the world first class, feeling the sun on my face, a particular fragrance I wore years back and so on. Putting all of them together, drives me constantly to do better in life so I can have more of those experiences. I have mentioned before on social media that my wallpaper on my computers are ideal properties I want to own and live in. They are very hard to purchase due to being out of my reach right now but not impossible to reach.

Here is an example:

You are going to make £1m in 2 years. For that (based on your own previous experience) you need to be strong enough to not waste time hanging around loser friends, not listen to negative parents and you need to want it more than anything else in the world. In your journey to success, you are going to constantly remind yourself of all the things that make you feel good and happy and will help you get there. The smell of Jasmine when you won that race, that song from Cafe Del Mar music when you made your first sale and took a holiday, the feeling of everyone telling you how great you did, that letter opener on your desk in your office you bought when in Venice on that great holiday and how looking at it now makes you feel happy etc

THE INITIAL DECISION

Before you start anything, you need to think about it extensively in your head. You need to do a lot of the fighting that you will be doing in the real world in your head first. I will repeat this again and agin but where you will fail will always be in your head. It will not be in the battleground of life out in the open. Your success and your failures are born, raised and live or die in your head. If you can control your mind, you can control the world around you. Success has NOTHING to do with the outside world because if you are strong enough, you can overcome anything.

Visualisation is all the rage these days and rightly so. Visualisation is basically you, putting yourself one step ahead by imagining the positive outcome that you hope to get. Sometimes it works a treat and other times it doesn't but the more you do it, the more chance of success you will have and the better you will get at it.

Let me ask you something. Why do you want to be successful? I mean REALLY? Give me one strong reason. Think about it. This reason needs to be bullet-proof; as simple as that, otherwise you are leaving yourself open to failure.

Let's take fat-loss as an example. You have the fat lady that has been fat all her life and on some sort of diet all her life and has tried and tried but somehow she never manages to become the slim person she aspires to be. She may have even lost a lot of weight at some stage but it always comes back to her being an overweight person. Why? Why can't she do it? And when she has success, why can't she keep to her new figure?

Let me give you a real life example. I knew this girl a few years back and she had an amazing body. She was into fitness and many people admired her and looked up to her. What they didn't know was that she used to be extremely obese. In fact, people who saw and admired her didn't know that deep down inside, she was petrified that she would get obese again and lived her life in fear, but for her, it was a good kind of fear.

Her decision to finally ditch her ways and get serious about losing weight came one night at 3 a.m. She desperately wanted to be a fitness competitor and to have a legacy and become a fitness personality and at that "talk with herself" at 3 a.m. she said enough is enough. She could not do this "being obese" any more. The next day she threw out all her food, threw out all her clothes and for her, the rest was history.

To be a fitness competitor, she had to change and stick to it. To remain a fitness personality and have a legacy, she needed to reach her goals and maintain her regime and keep going. As I write this book, she is still going strong some 20 years later. She is still going at it because that initial reason and that "snapping point" was so strong that there was no turning back. It was the beginning of the end for her and the fact that she wanted a continuation of her initial goal (legacy) meant that she had to carry on with her new lifestyle.

In the example above you have all the ingredients of success. Whether life or financial success, you will get there if you have:

1. That initial strong, unshakable, "enough is enough" reason to start something new and different from what you have been doing and

2. An indestructible reason why you need to carry on despite anything that may happen around you at any time, no matter how many things or how many times.

If you can get the above 2 right for "you" in business or any other endeavour you have been struggling with, then nothing will stop you. You will start something ASAP and you will not be put off or side-tracked from ultimate success.

Don't start anything until you have your mindset right

Mindset is SO important in starting a profitable business that you are strongly advised NOT to start anything until you are 100% certain of the reason why you are going into a business of your own and 100% certain that the reason is so strong that it will stand any test, short of death! I mean it!

I have had close relatives dying but the next day I have been back at work because I had things to do. I know it sounds terrible to some of you. Does it? If so, then maybe you are not cut out for the cut-throat world that is the business world.

You may of course get lucky and not need to have a strong reason or be as harsh as me but what if? What if your chosen business did end up having lots of competitors, lots of problems and you were not mentally prepared for it? What then? Well, by that time you are well and truly screwed because you didn't take the right steps in the first place in ensuring that your mind-set is right and that you are truly the warrior you need to be to make it in business, become profitable and end up a success story.

Battles are not won on battlegrounds. They are not won in boardrooms, bedrooms or in the streets. Battles are always won in the minds of those who fight. How else could you explain a small guy beating a big guy? A 200 man army, beating an army of thousands? A small company growing from nothing and sinking a much bigger rival? If you can master your own mind, you are a true warrior; one that is very hard to defeat, one that will carry on no matter what and won't fear anyone or anything.

WHY PROFIT IS SO IMPORTANT

Let's talk a little about profit. Firstly, don't compare your business to others. You don't know their circumstances, so start your own business from scratch and follow your own path. Be your own competitor and don't get distracted with others, their business and their success or lack thereof.

Is turnover more important or profit? Surely many different business people would give you a different answer. I can only tell you from my own experience and profit is the essence of any business.

LET'S START WITH A SIMPLE EXAMPLE.

A. Say you bought a phone case for £1 and sold it for £2. In a month you sold 100, so that would give you £200 turnover and £100 profit.

B. Say you sold it for £1.20 but you sold 300 (more turnover). That will give you £320 turnover, which to some is much better but your profit will be only £60.

The higher turnover is very good for cashflow of course but now, you have got rid of 300 items, so you need to buy another 300 to replace the ones sold and you have only made a profit of £60.

In example B, out of your £320 turnover, you need to spend £300 to buy more covers, leaving you with £20.

In example A, out of £200 turnover, you need to spend £100 to buy more covers, leaving you with £100.

The above is a very basic example; in reality many rules come into play when it comes to calculating profit and turnover: the actual profit margin, whether you are preparing your business for a sale, your tax status, competition, price of transport/products/wages etc. are all factors that we will be discussing shortly. This is why business is a maze and not so easy to get into or to navigate!

However, if you stick to one basic rule, you should be OK! Yes, you really can simplify all the complex formulas of business and whether you should do this or that to one simple formula and that is:

Make sure profit is at the heart of your entire business and ensure you make the maximum amount possible in profit.

I repeat: the maximum amount possible. I say this, so there is no come-backs. People ask whether they should really make so much (if they are in a good industry)? Is it right? Others aren't doing it, so why should they? Isn't it dishonest to make so much money? Will god punish them? I mean, seriously!

It's true that if you have no cashflow, you are going to struggle and your business will not survive for very long. However if you have no profit, you have no long-term business. You can go on for a while and rob Peter to pay Paul but eventually, it will all catch up with you and you will find yourself, unable to pay suppliers or anyone.

Loss of turnover is a fast death whereas loss of profit or lack of profit is a slow, painful death. The problem with not having good profit is that all can look rosy and great and you can even see yourself as a "proper businessman" when suddenly BAM - you're totally done for! FINISHED! Suddenly, you realise you can't find the money to pay people. At least with having bad cashflow, you know you are in trouble. When you have little or no profit, you may be completely oblivious to the fact that your business is dying.

This is why it is always better to start slow, start small and start smart and that means starting with a business that is highly profitable, even if small - as profitable as you can make it.

If I had the choice between a very high turnover, low profit business and a much smaller high profit business I would choose the high profit one. It is easier to manage, you know you are far from ever getting in trouble and you can scale up smartly if you so choose. A high turnover, relatively low profit margin business is a handful.

My ideas in this book are not written in stone and obviously they come from my own experiences, some of the people I have worked with and those I see around me. When your business is profitable a few things happen:

1. You can always buy more stock/product/services.

2. You can pay people on time.

3. You can have a good line of credit, should you need it.

4. You can plan ahead and have breathing space.

5. You don't get caught out with tax or other big value items in the future.

6. You can allocate money to marketing of your products/services.

7. You can build a proper brand and not be forced into selling cheap.

At the end of the day, every business-person's dream is to have a profitable business, proper brand and something that will give them money, not give them stress and allow them to live the life they dream of. A profitable business can do that. Problems arise when a) the profit or turnover is not enough or b) things change. For example, you marry a money-grabbing wife who wants to shop all the time! Or your competitor cuts all prices and you end up not making any sales or profit.

If you are smart and have started a very profitable business, many things can take you away from this path and make you start concentrating on turnover rather than profit. My advice is, don't do it. If you have a good brand/business with good profit margins, you need to stick to the basic rule which is "maximum profit".

We will be discussing all of this a little bit later on.

PASSION

Let's talk about passion. Anything that you do has to have passion behind it otherwise even if you are successful at the beginning you may not very well carry it through to ultimate success. In business, there are two paths you can take. One is if you're passionate about something and you start a business out of your passion and somehow you get it going and you make a success of it. The other alternative is to do something that you are not passionate about but you end up making money out of it. This is a more difficult route to take because it becomes more mechanical and you may find it harder to carry on with that business because there is no deep passion for the product or services that you are offering.

In an ideal scenario you should have a mixture of both so you should be in a business that you are passionate about and that you are passionate about the products and the services AND something that is mechanical in the way it produces money for you and gives you a profit and enables you to have the life that you want to live and possibly have an exit strategy in the end.

Examples of something that is passion-driven could be if for example you like football and you set up a football academy. You could train a few people, you could train children, you could train teenagers to become good footballers or you could think even bigger and make franchises of it and and make money out of the franchise and grow bigger and you could think even bigger and eventually sell the whole business for an exit.

You would be very lucky to have a business that is passion-driven. Don't get me wrong, lots of people have businesses that are driven by passion but usually they are not very successful businesses because their passion is not necessarily a big money spinner or innovative or new or something that would catch on and grow like wildfire.

Whilst it could be for some people, for most, it is not a good route to become rich by following your passion because people who usually start businesses because of their passion are actually not real business people; they are just passionate about what they're doing and are not necessarily business-minded.

On the other hand people who start a business because they have a good idea can do well. So, if you're very lucky, ideally you want to have a business which combines both ingredients: 1) something that you are passionate about and 2) something that is new/innovative and can end up making you a lot of money in the long run.

Let's say you stumble across carbon fibre phone cases and no one else is doing them and you find a way of making money out of them such as by selling on Amazon. You may not be passionate about carbon fibre or phones or technical stuff but you keep going during hard times because you are making money. Hopefully if you're reading this book, then you are passionate about money and making money, so that can and usually does become the passion of people who start something that they may not necessarily have an actual interest in.

You never know where a good money-making idea can come from, so you mustn't be rigid about it. It can come from your passion, it can come from a good idea, it can come from you seeing something somewhere, maybe at a trade fair or it can come from you having worked somewhere or for someone and learnt something that nobody else knows. It can be a tweak of something that already exists and you bettering that or it can be an innovation in itself.

One of my friends used to be an estate agent and for many years he worked as an estate agent and I really didn't put him down as an entrepreneur type at all because I knew him as an estate agent. He stumbled across a new idea to do with cars; he was no expert in cars. He left his job and risked everything for this new car idea because it was very innovative and no one else was doing it and he had a great product and he ended up doing great marketing for it and his business grew and grew and grew.

After a while he did become very passionate about what he was doing because a) it was providing him with a lot of money and b) he started to get more and more into the product he was selling so he had no choice but to learn more about it and eventually become passionate about it. Many people have tried to copy him and his business model because they have seen the huge success that he has achieved but because he was one of the first and he keeps innovating, not many people have caught up with him.

DON'T GET DISCOURAGED

The biggest obstacle people face when they are thinking of starting a business or if they have started one and is not doing very well is that they get discouraged. This can be internal discouragement in that their own mind is defeating them or external discouragement from friends family or people that they know or don't know and the opinion that they give.

Discouragement is one of the biggest factors why many businesses fail and it is something that can easily be tackled by doing a variety of things such as positive thinking, not listening to other people, being consistent, having a plan, having goals and milestones, and rewarding yourself. There are lots and lots of books on motivation out there that you can read. This word "discouragement" doesn't necessarily show up in the title of books but discouragement is really lack of motivation, so you can choose to read about motivation to learn about discouragement.

Many people don't have the internal flame that keeps burning and burning when they start a business because at the end of the day, they are human beings and human beings are prone to emotions and are fragile. But you have to see yourself as a machine when you start a business and you have to see yourself as a strong machine that has to carry on and carry on until you become successful; there is no space for discouragement or doubt.

You can try and model yourself on someone very successful that you know or that you've seen and if you ever feel discouraged, just say to yourself what would they do? This is a good way of tackling obstacles, especially if you don't know what to do, you can look at your role model and think what would they do?

HERE ARE SOME WAYS TO TACKLE DISCOURAGEMENT:

1. Have an end goal which is realistic and achievable but bigger than one that can easily be achieved. It needs to be achievable, otherwise discouragement may kick in.

2. Make sure you have some milestones along the way that you can tick off when you've achieved them.

3. Reward yourself along the way; it doesn't have to be a car or a house or something very expensive but it is good to reward yourself when you've achieved something, just so you feel good about it and it can also act as an anchor for success.

4. Surround yourself with positive people. Positive people will encourage you and will see your vision and help you along the way. Negative people are one of the biggest reasons why so many people get discouraged. These days they call negative people haters. Whatever you want to call them, they should not be in your life because they could be causing your discouragement and

could be one of the biggest factors why you don't do well in your life or in your business.

5. Never compare yourself to other people; remember you are your own competition and you are not there to compete with everyone else or every other company. At the end of the day there is always someone richer than you, more successful than you, stronger than you, faster than you and more innovative than you. If you were to compete with every person around then you would be very frustrated and extremely discouraged.

6. There is the old saying that says the glass is either half full or half empty. This is such a good way of looking at things because many people look at the glass half empty and that can lead to discouragement whereas if you were to look at the glass half full and see everything that you have achieved, then you would be encouraged to carry on and do more. Rome wasn't built in a day and this is very true; if you try to tackle something very big, your mind may work against you and discourage you. It is always better to do things in a smaller way and achieve smaller things on your way to a much bigger goal.

7. Without failure there would be no success, without failure, life would not be as sweet or as pleasurable and would be extremely boring. Winston Churchill had a good saying, he said "success consists of going from failure to failure without loss of enthusiasm". You should remember that because lots and lots of people fail and they fail more than once or twice or 10 times or even a hundred times but truly successful people are those who will get up and will carry on and on until they achieve their ultimate goal and until they do better today than they did yesterday, which is you doing better today than you did yesterday; that should be your goal.

8. In Neurolinguistic Programming (NLP) they say that whatever

happens to you is not important; it is how you perceive it and how you react to it that is extremely important and it is your perception that makes the experience pleasant or unpleasant. This is so important and one of the ways that you can actually stop discouragement and tackle it in the right way. Let's say if you ran a race and you came last, you could say to yourself that you came last and you are pathetic and weak and not good at competitions. Or you could say to yourself that you took part which is more than what can be said about most other people, and that you had the drive and determination and motivation to actually take part in the race and coming last can only get you better and you can only do better from that point. It is really how you see it that is important and not what actually happens to you.

9. The majority of successful people whether in business or in other areas of life such as in acting or arts or entertainment have had a whole variety of failures adding up to thousands of failures before they tasted success. Failure is not an option so your only option is finding ways of overcoming failure.

PRODUCTS VERSUS SERVICE

So you want to start a profitable business and you really don't know where to start. Should you bring out a product? Should you start some sort of service? Should you do both, maybe have a product and service?

This really is the million-dollar question, isn't it? And whatever you start, you may very well end up doing it for many many years, so you really need to think long and hard about it and you really cannot rush into this because whatever you do can become a very big part of your life and if you have a family, it can become a big part of your family's life.

The best place to start is obviously with yourself if you have a skill or inside knowledge or something that is different from others in terms of a service you can offer; you may very well want to think about that. Is it something you're passionate about? Is it something that you can make a lot of money out of? Only you would know those things but if you are service-minded and many people are, then you may want to get into some sort of service.

The limitations of doing a service-based business are obviously that you may not be able to turn over a lot of money from it but there are ways around that such as franchising or employing more people. Examples of service businesses are things like personal training, accountancy, consultancy, or any sort of personal service.

Services usually do have a ceiling as opposed to products, so unless you actually have something in the service industry that is very unique, then your business may well need to be a product-based business. Products have the advantage of being very fluid in that you can sell them to a small market or to a larger market or you can bring out complementary products or different products or bigger products and do lots with them.

You can of course combine products and services, so for example you can start a small gym where you offer the services of personal trainers, where you offer the use of products in the form of equipment and where you offer sports nutrition for people who work out and healthy food for them to eat. If you're very ambitious you can open another gym and another one and another one smashing the ceiling that could exist in a service-type industry.

If you look around some of the richest people in the world, usually what they do is product-based unless if they are in an industry such as financial services or banking. And this is not bad news really because once you find the right product and you market it the right way, things that you will be learning in this book, then you can end up becoming extremely wealthy and live the life that you dream of.

START WITH YOUR GOAL

I often talk about your map and why you need a map and why you need a destination for everything that you do in order to become successful. The example I give is someone arriving in a new city and the choices are: that person not knowing where they're going which is the worst thing or knowing where they're going but not knowing how to get there. In business you need to 1st and foremost know exactly where you're going. This is extremely important; so if you've arrived in Rome, then you can say to yourself that you are going to the Colosseum for example. That is your goal and that is where all your energies and efforts should be concentrated towards; this is extremely important because without a goal you will be lost in all areas of life not just business (or Rome!).

Whatever business you plan to start, you need to have a goal. Is your goal to turn over £1 million in the next year? Is your goal to turn over a hundred thousand pounds? What is your exact goal? That goal is your Colosseum; that goal is your destination. That goal is where everything in your power has to be concentrated towards to get you there in the quickest possible time.

The profit versus turnover debate comes into action here because your goal could be to have a company with huge turnover, very little profit but ready for an eventual sale. Or your goal could be to have a company with a product or service that is very profitable and just gives you an amazing lifestyle for many many years to come; so everything that you're doing in business is dependent upon your main goal.

This is why it's so important before you do anything whatsoever that you set your goal in your head and write it clearly on a piece of paper and that goal cannot change. It is important for you to take your time and decide what is your goal in business and where do you want to end up in one year, five years, 10 years 20 years' time.

Your goal will dictate whether you should go into services, bring out a product and what direction you should take and also what industry you should go into. If you really do not have a clue at this stage, then don't start your business yet. Now, I am hoping that most of you have some sort of idea as to where you want to go and what you want to do. Don't worry if you don't because that's the whole purpose of this book; it is to teach you how to start a successful and profitable business even if you have no business experience or ideas or know which industry you want to be in.

It doesn't hurt to start writing down what your main goal is by going into business; this is a very important document. Make sure you get a pen and paper and you write it down right now. We have touched on this already with the Yacht example; here we are getting more into the practical aspects of making sure your business is going to be profitable.

WHICH INDUSTRIES SHOULD YOU WORK IN?

The reference to passion comes into play here because obviously the industry you may want to choose is what you are passionate about or an industry where you have inside knowledge on or an industry where you've stumbled across an innovative new product or something that you think can make you a lot of money.

This is why it is so important to keep your eyes and ears open and see what's new and check out all the latest trends. Alibaba.com has a section with all new trends that you can always look at and see what product is trending. News stories also give you an idea of what is trending and popular. You can also look at the rich list and see what businesses have made the most money for people.

My earliest businesses were always connected to what I was passionate about. I started buying and selling cars in my teens (I love cars), then I became a Reflexologist (I love health), I started a sports nutrition business (I love nutrition) and I invested in property (I love luxury properties). These are just some examples but enough to demonstrate to you that I have always got myself involved in things I have been very passionate about. You should think about this for yourself.

The industry you go into is extremely important and as important as whether you should have a product or service because it can become a big part of your life and it needs to be something that holds your interest by you being passionate about it or holds your interest by you making a lot of money in it. For example if you don't like diesel or the smell of diesel but you find a product that is associated with the diesel industry then you may struggle because you don't like the smell of diesel, you are not passionate about it and you don't want to be in that industry.

You may be anxious and you may be impatient about starting your own business but sometimes it may be worthwhile to just pause and delay it until you come up with a very good idea. Alternatively you can always work for someone that has got a lot of good ideas or someone that has a successful business and you can learn from them and then try and emulate them by coming up with something that can make you wealthy.

Once again the point has to be emphasised that you are not in competition with anybody but yourself and you cannot look at other people who may have been successful at 18 or 20 or 25 and if you are say in your 30s, get frustrated. You are only competing with yourself and you have to remember that and not get frustrated by it. Everybody has their own destiny and everybody has to follow their own path.

As general guidance, if you're really lost as to whether you should do a product or service or which industry you should go to, then look at whatever that to you seems very successful and that someone else is doing and emulate them. Copy them and try and better what they are doing or do it in a way that is different to how they are doing it. There's nothing wrong with that because at the end of the day, everything is a copy of something else. Go with your instinct but do work it out in your head first.

A lot of the times, you will know when you have come across the right product or the right business idea. It's a little bit like when you come across your future wife or husband, you kind of know and you feel confident and you know exactly what to do and you almost feel at peace. Sometimes it's better not to stress or worry about what product you will be bringing out. As long as you're out there researching, looking around, keeping your eyes and ears open, sooner or later you will come across the right idea and the right product that can make you extremely rich. Persistence will always pay off, for some sooner, for others a little bit later.

MARKET RESEARCH

The best thing you can do before you go into any sort of product launch or service launch or your new business is to do lots and lots and lots of market research. Market research is asking the right questions from a whole variety of general people. The whole point of market research is not to go there with a specific end goal but try and get unbiased opinion on the road you're about to embark on. You need independent, unbiased opinions and information.

Successful people do lots of market research and testing and gather a lot of data and analyse that data over and over again. By doing market research you end up having a great deal of data that can be useful to you in the initial stages of whether you should launch at all or later, on how to brand, market and develop your idea. Just as you need to be patient with finding the right idea, you also need to be patient before launching it and you need to do market research.

These days because of social media and the Internet, it is very easy to do market research. You really don't need to go out there with a pad and pen and stand outside the train station and ask lots of people lots of questions! You can easily set up a social media page and once you have some following in the specific area that you want to embark on, you can just ask them whatever question you need to ask to do your market research. That's the beauty of today's age and that a lot of the things that used to be very difficult in the past, are extremely easy and can often be done with speed.

FINDING YOUR IDEAL PRODUCT

A good way of finding a product for yourself is to look on alibaba.com or aliexpress.com and find products that seem to have a good profit margin that you could sell in your own country, possibly online. This is an example really but it gives you an idea of the kind of stuff you could do. So let's say if you find a keyring made of titanium and it's cheap on alibaba.com and you think you can sell it in your country to shops or online at a profit, then you should get in touch with the supplier and try and negotiate a good price and try and get some made for you or just get some generic ones and have them shipped over. If you have no money to start with at all, then you can create a free online shop, market the product you find interesting and when you have a sale, place your order with the supplier on alibaba.com. The disadvantage here is time-scale for receipt of goods to the final customer.

You can sell things at a profit and with that money you can buy more key-rings or different kind of products from the same supplier or somewhere else. I'm really generalising but you can find products anywhere; you can find furniture in a local market in France or you can find cheap products online in China or you may find something just local to you that is cheap and you could potentially sell it more expensively somewhere else.

These days a lot of people set up online shops and they sell things very easily. Your choice for your business can be what millions of others aspire to do or already doing which is this buying something cheap somewhere and selling it online at a profit somewhere else. There are lots of podcasts, books and places where you can learn how to market and how to drive traffic to your website selling products. Technology is moving so fast that probably by the time you read this, there is a new social media platform that allows you to do cheap advertising and drive traffic to your website and you really need to be patient to see exactly what works. Right now, one of the best places to drive traffic and customers to your site is Facebook advertising. I rank it much higher than Twitter, Snapchat or Google Adwords.

HOW TO START ADVERTISING YOUR PRODUCTS/ SERVICES

At the end of the day, you want to pay the least amount to get the most revenue back. That is the idea with most advertising and you would make a mistake if you were to just start spending and spending without knowing where you are spending your money and without knowing exactly how much your spend is bringing you back in revenue.

Whether you are doing online marketing or sales or you have a shop or you have any other business, the fundamental principles are the same, which are: you must spend the least amount of money to get the most amount of revenue. Where most people go wrong is that they either don't keep track of their money and don't look carefully at their spend versus the revenue or they just spend and spend without any thought as to whether that money is actually bringing in revenues. Of course there is something to be said for brand awareness but personally I think it's always better to account for every penny spent and to ensure that money you spend on advertising is giving actual monetary returns to you. This way you just cannot go wrong.

As an example, very clever people will set up several Facebook campaigns with very little spend and will track those campaigns for a few days or even a few weeks and sometimes even a few months to see which exact campaign is bringing in the most revenue.

They then go on and select that particular high returns campaign and spend the money on that and nothing else. In an ideal scenario you want to be spending as little as possible to bring the most amount of revenue. Back in the day when Google advertising first started I personally used to spend 10p to drive traffic to my businesses. 10p was the maximum I allowed for myself and it was very profitable until more and more players came on board and Google started to charge more for many keywords as a result of the excess competition. So it started to get extremely expensive for some keywords. I remember that I stopped advertising with Google AdWords when one particular keyword shot up to £30 per click and I just thought that was really crazy. Imagine spending 10p to get a customer and then that shooting up to £30 to get the customer; well there's a big difference and sometimes you need to be smart with your money and take your money elsewhere when there is too much competition.

THE ESSENCE OF BRANDING

Once you have a product or service, you will want to be spending money on a variety of things such as advertising and marketing. But before you go to do any of that and before you even start to launching your product or service, the most important thing you should think about is branding. Branding is really a one-way road where there is no return and once you've embarked upon that road you better be sure as to where you're going because turning back is almost impossible and even if it was possible, it can cost you a lot in money and can cost you loss of customers.

Your brand is everything that your product and service is about, ideally told to the customer in one second. Your brand should tell the customer everything about your business in a heartbeat. Your brand is your logo, the colour of your logo, your tagline, the look and feel of your logo and any distinctive characteristics of your logo. Your brand is how your business is perceived by someone who looks at it without knowing anything about your product or service.

You really need to think about your brand and how you want to appear to the outside world. For example if you are selling cheap products, the “stack them high sell them cheap” type and you are looking to attract a certain demographic, then your colours and the look and feel of your brand has to sit well with that demographic. If you have a cheap brand, then there is no point using colours such as black and gold with fonts that give the impression of luxury and opulence. Because this will confuse the customer and will not serve you well.

On the other hand if your brand is an exclusive premium, high end brand then you must be very careful with your branding and things such as your logo and you must avoid using cheap colours, fonts and a look that will confuse your customer or devalue your brand (not that it has any value at the outset lol). High end people are used to seeing a certain look and feel about the brands that they buy into and they are very wary of cheap-looking brands. It is very important for you to brand your product or service exactly as how you wanted to be perceived. This will all affect profits.

This is where investment in a good designer is extremely well worth the spend. You need to sit down with the designer and decide exactly what message you are trying to give to the people out there and before you start your journey to a highly profitable business, before you start marketing your product, before you start doing anything, you must get your branding right.

Imagine a High Street where every shop is a cheap shop selling £1 goods or maximum £5 goods and there are no expensive shops there and the people visiting that High Street are not very rich and don't have a great deal of disposable income. Now imagine a shop coming along and doing a carbon fibre sign with gold lettering and doing something that is totally out of character with that high street and at the same time selling cheap products like the other shops on that High Street. What do you think would happen? What would happen is that not many people will go into that shop because they will be confused by the brand and the brand message, regardless of what that shop is selling.

WHO IS YOUR CUSTOMER?

In order to be able to design your brand and your brand's message, the first question you must ask yourself is who exactly is your customer? This is the most important question you can ask yourself before you can even do your branding. And it is a question that many people fail to ask themselves before they start a business and it is a question that will guide you throughout your business life and will guide you when times are hard and when things are going bad.

Imagine knowing exactly who your customer is, imagine knowing their routines, imagine knowing their spending habits, imagine knowing their hobbies, imagine knowing everything about them. Wouldn't that be beautiful? Well, you can do this by deciding exactly who your customer is, in terms of their income, their hobbies what they are looking for, why they would buy your product, why they wouldn't buy your product, and everything else that will decide why they would be interested in your product. Decide your ideal customer at the outset.

Once you know who your customer is and you've decided on

that, you cannot change that in the future. Because your entire branding, marketing and advertising will be based on that very central question of who exactly is your customer. For example, in one of my businesses I sell to very wealthy individuals who have great disposable income and can afford my product regardless of price or economic uncertainties. Imagine that?

This is such a beautiful place to be, because you know exactly who you're going after and you know exactly who you can ignore or not be bothered about. I know this sounds a bit bad to most people, however you really do not need to worry about other "non customers" once you know who your customer is. In my businesses, I really did not worry about customers who didn't have a huge income and who could not afford my product because they were not my customer and chances were even if they could have afforded my product, they probably would not have been happy or they would not come back because they could not afford it in the first place.

Please sit down and have a good think once you've decided on your product or service, about exactly who is going to be your ideal customer.

TASK

Write down 10 characteristics of your ideal customer. They can be anything from the way they look to the way they sound, to the way they dress, to their hobbies, to their income, to their career path, to their religion and anything else that you think relevant. In fact this is a very productive exercise and you may very well want to spend some time doing it and some people even go further and they get someone to draw their ideal customer in the form of a real-looking male and/or female.

As much as it sounds funny, it is actually not and will really guide you to focus as to who is your ideal customer and what branding, advertising and marketing you should do to entice that customer. Once it is a real-looking person, it is much easier to get your imagination going.

Coming back to the essence of branding, everything rests on what product or service you are selling and who is your ideal customer and once you find a good designer that you really trust, then make sure that you sit down with them and try and get your branding right. Make sure before you hire them that you have seen examples of their work. Once they are hired, you must get them to give you a number of designs that you can then choose one from and you can both start perfecting that design.

I will emphasise again, branding is a one-way road and it is very very difficult to change your brand at some stage in the future. I remember one of my main competitors had the word muscle in their name for many many years and they had a lot of customers and the brand was very strong. Once they were bought by a much bigger company, the company decided to replace the word muscle with the word nutrition in the brand name. Imagine this huge company with all the resources in the world tried to change the essence of this newly acquired brand and they actually failed miserably at doing it. This was because they didn't stick to the first rule of branding which is you can't change your brand at a later stage - you may possibly tweak it but you cannot change it dramatically, so you better get it right in the first place.

A GOOD EXAMPLE OF SIMPLE BRANDING THAT MADE ONE BUSINESS MILLIONS

There is a very big garbage company in America that turns over millions of dollars and it is a very good example of the power of branding. There are lots of garbage collection companies in America. However this particular garbage company decided to give itself a very good brand image a friendly nice sounding name that made itself look like a company easy to deal with and a big player in the industry. Their brand became very well-known and soon they had many franchises and as a result of proper branding, the company is now a multi-multi-million pound garbage collection company across America and a huge part of that is due to the fact that they decided to really spend some time and effort branding their business.

Branding is not just a logo; their particular branding is about the logo, the trucks, the friendly bright green colour of the logo, the way they brand their trucks, the shirts of the people that work for them and the packaging they use. Everything about the company reinforces the brand theme and the brand colours.

Some of the biggest companies in the world have some of the most recognisable brands and logos and if you pay close attention, you will see that as simple as it looks, a great deal of effort has been spent on them. Think yellow and red and what brand do you think about? Chances are you think of McDonald's. Think of a tick and you will think about Nike. Think of an apple and you will think about Apple, the computer brand. Think of red and white and you will probably think of Coca-Cola. You see the power of branding gets into your conscious and your subconscious and the same applies to your customers, so if you can get your branding really right, you are onto a great thing in terms of having short-term and long-term sales and customer loyalty, retention and recommendation.

To conclude this section about branding, you must spend as much as you can afford on the best possible brand expert or designer you can get your hands on, to get your branding right and you must be sure as to who exactly is your customer and who you are going to serve and who you are going to deal with and most importantly who you are not going to deal with.

Becoming successful in business and having a profitable business is all about focus and knowing exactly where you're going. This is why knowing your customer and creating your brand in accordance with the customer is part of that knowing exactly where you're going. Your business life is going to be so easy once you've set these important principles in place.

START EARLY IF YOU CAN, BECAUSE PRACTICE MAKES PERFECT

You have to start somewhere in business and many people start early on in life. You've all heard of the stories of the boy that sells sweets to his friends in school and soon enough he has other boys working for him selling sweets and he starts making money from an early age. I say sweets but I'm sure many children sell other things such as things in demand, including drugs which is the same business principle, albeit illegal and immoral! The entrepreneurial spirit is the same nonetheless, although the moral compass may be somewhat questionable.

If you have been someone who started out early selling things to your friends or at least trying to succeed in business, then that is a good sign. It shows that you are determined and interested in an entrepreneurial life and not interested in working for others. Well and truly never ever be discouraged by failure as hard as it feels and as painful as it can be. Failure is what makes true warriors, failure is what gives you that experience to go on to bigger things; failure is part of the process that many successful people have experienced over the course of human existence.

In many ways, business and business principles are very simple if not for other outside factors that come in to complicate things, such as competition, rising costs, personal problems or a changing world or economy. The simple principle is the principle of selling sweets to your friends in school. You may go to a cash-and-carry and buy a whole load of sweets and then you take them to school where there are no sweet shops and when your friends want some sweets and have no access to them, you can sell them the sweets. This gives you profit. You can make even more profit by buying the sweets a lot cheaper and selling them a lot more expensive, for example when your friends are very hungry or when they are very far from a sweet shop, such as on a field trip outside of school. The principles are very simple; you need to buy cheap and you need to sell expensive and you need to make sure that the environment and circumstances are so that there are conductive to you selling at maximum profit. If you can control the environment, even better!

It sounds so simple, doesn't it? If only all businesses were as simple as selling sweets to your friends at school. Let's stick with the sweet analogy for now and let's see what can go wrong in this situation. The cash-and-carry can put its prices up, reducing your profit or eliminating it altogether. The cash-and-carry, your supplier, can go out of business and basically kill your supply line. The Principal of the school can find out about your sweet selling and ban you from selling sweets, a little bit like a regulatory body from the government banning your products later on in life. There could be other boys or girls starting to sell sweets at a cheaper price, a little bit like competitors trying to take you out. There could be a problem with your sweets and people stop buying from you. You could get ill and not go to school for a while and someone else can take over your business and sell to the kids and by the time you come back you will have no business left.

As you can see the same things that can go wrong in real life in business can go wrong in a small scenario of selling sweets to your friends. This is why it is so important to be very profitable as early as possible in this sweet selling scenario, so that way you can start saving money or investing it in your sweet business to make sure you don't go out of business. For example you can have an alternative sweet manufacturer, you could bribe the Principal so he doesn't ban you (I'm being serious!) or you could do special deals for your customers so they don't go to anybody else.

In fact the principles and experiences that many school kids go through whilst selling things to their friends in school go on to become important principles in their world of business later in life. If you haven't been someone who has sold sweets to their friends then don't worry because this book is about telling you those simple but very important principles that ensure you stay in business and you stay profitable.

PLANNING IS EVERYTHING

Many people come to me wanting help with the beginning of their business asking how or where they can get some money from to start their business journey. There are many places you can get money from such as banks, relatives, government grants, personal loans, savings and funds set up to help businesses. The reality however is no one is going to give you money unless you can prove that you are not going to waste their money and that you will do good with that money.

Whether you are going to a bank manager or a relative, you need to prove that you are really serious about your business and that you have planned everything in advance and you can show that your business will get off the ground, stay profitable and give them their money without you risking their money. You need to write down all your costs including actual cost of product or service, shipping, packaging, office hire, transport, storage, mortgage repayments, tax bill, labelling, staff costs and anything and everything that will cost you money.

You also need to calculate exactly how much you're planning on turning over in the year but also breaking it down to monthly, weekly and daily amounts. Many people plan way more ahead than just a year. However a year is a good time to show people what you can do. On a very basic level profit is your retail price, taking away all your costs. This is your profit. This is called gross profit which is what you sell something at minus what it cost you to buy. Then you have net profit which is your real profit taking all costs including tax into account. Some people don't bring tax into net profit whilst others do; for me not bringing tax into net profit is absolutely crazy. You must know what your exact net profit is which includes taxation.

The problem with tax is that it is not paid straightaway and so, many people don't bring it into the equation of business and that is wrong because you have to pay it sooner or later and just because you have to pay it sometime in the future does not mean that you must ignore it. In fact many businesses have sunk as a result of not taking taxation into account in their profit and loss scenario or in their initial business plan.

You must remember that costs will always go up, whilst taxation may remain the same. Even if your manufacturer insists to you that the cost of goods will be passed on to you whether they go up or down, chances are that they will never pass on a saving to you even if their raw ingredient prices go down. Everybody is in it to make money and if you are smart, you will be doing exactly the same thing. This is why I tell you that you must make the maximum amount of profit from day one and by maximum I mean as much as possible. Because you have to bear in mind that costs will always go up and even if you're making a thousand percent today, that profit in the future may very well dwindle down to 50% or much less (even a loss) depending on your industry.

A great business plan is one which shows the potential investor that you will be making an incredible amount of profit and even if they were to pick holes in your plan and say that you are wrong about this or that, once they see that there is a huge profit margin in your business they will have faith in you.

Profit is like a safety net. Imagine you're an acrobat and you have a 1 m x 1 m safety net underneath you. Well, that is not a huge safety net and if you fall on either side you may get hurt. However if your safety net was 20 m x 20 m then the chances are that wherever you fall you won't get hurt. In business you are aiming to have the maximum possible safety net at all times around you. This safety net is high profits and it ensures that you never get hurt and you never fall and you are always safe in your business life.

WHAT IS A GOOD PROFIT?

A good profit to one person may be a terrible profit to someone else. Going back to what I was saying earlier, you cannot compare yourself to other people or compare your business to other businesses (I know, I keep repeating this). Every business is different and every business is an individual entity in itself. The question of what is a good profit is also very much dependent on the ambitions of the proprietor of that business. To some people a 10% or 30% profit is more than enough in giving them longevity in their business and helping them have a nice life. To others going below 3000% is a scary thought and they would not enter a business unless it had crazy amounts of profit.

If you're at the outset of the business my advice will always remain the same which is start a business that has a lot of profit in it and set your profit at the maximum amount you can possibly make. As your business grows the chances are that your profit margin will get lower and lower, as it happens with many businesses. Of course you can find ways of increasing your profit margin, perhaps by branching into other areas or reducing costs or increasing your price.

You have to be realistic depending on what business you are doing. Some businesses cannot make 3000% or even a hundred percent profit whereas some businesses can make even more. Take an online study course for example, once the principal has created it, if the price is extremely high as many are, then the profits can be quite high. Compare this against a newsagents where the owner buys products from a local cash-and-carry and most products have a set retail price and the business cannot sell for a higher profit; and typically all newsagents will have set costs such as rent or mortgage, staff and other predictable costs. So a newsagents for example may only ever be able to make a maximum 30% margin and never any more. The problem here is that rents may go up, price of products may go up, and other things such as the cost of wages for staff may go up, reducing profits.

If you are a personal trainer, you can only charge a certain amount. You can charge more if you were to enter a niche market for example or you can take more courses and become more qualified and charge more; however, generally you will have a profit margin with a set limit. The only way you can change your profit margin is by being creative, better branding or using advertising methods such as recommendations which don't require you to spend any money. A personal trainer is a good example of a business that has a set margin but can change his fortunes with the smart application of the aforementioned.

Personal trainers can also expand but this is the sort of thing that starts eating into the margins of a business. For example advertising to grow, training new personal trainers, travel time and travel costs and spending time on other things such as meetings. This is why I was saying earlier you have to make the decision whether you want to go into products or services and you have to decide on your profit margin. It is interesting to think that many people don't think the profit margin is their decision, they think it's something that comes along as a part of the business. I really do not think this is the case because when you start from the bottom and you decide what industry you want to go into and how you wish to brand your product or services, you can have full control over your margin at least at the outset. You can have a more or less controllable profit margin especially if you start with a business that has a high profit margin to begin with and you stick to certain business principles.

Manufacturing is another example where profit margins are usually set but can vary depending on how the end product is marketed. You can manufacture for the bottom of the market where everything is cheap and price sensitive thereby giving you very low margins but potentially reaching the masses or you can manufacture for a niche or a high-end clientele and make a lot more profit. This sort of high profit is usually as a result of great marketing, branding, advertising and brand control. Brand control is something that is very important if you are in a high margin business whether be it personal services or products. If you dilute your brand and lose control of it then the chances are your profit margin will suffer greatly. This is something that I have learnt first hand in a number of my businesses and it has been a painful and valuable lesson. If you lose control of your brand, then you lose control of your profit margin, so it is extremely important to always do good for your brand and never lose control of it.

Another example that I can give you is that of estate agents. You have the estate agents at the high end selling the very expensive houses and charging great commission and then you have some new entries into the market who will charge as little as £500 to sell a house for you. Which one makes more money? You would think the high-end estate agent that charges thousands of pounds would make more money however this very much depends on their costs which can be astronomical. So if you were to start an estate agency you would ask yourself the question: where do you want to be in terms of branding and who will your clientele be and that will guide you to your profit margin and eventual costs.

There are ways you can control your profit margin and maintain a high profit margin and the way you can do that is to stay ahead of the game by innovation and cost reduction. For example taking the example of and estate agent, back in the day they used to have to pay quite a lot of money to advertise in magazines and newspapers, before the various online platforms for advertising properties came along. The cost saving from having to advertise in a magazine or newspaper down to a few pounds for online advertising can be dramatic. In fact the Internet age and social media has helped many businesses reduce costs and reach a much wider audience especially if they embrace the new technology and take the time to understand and learn it in a practical and correct way.

I don't want to sound gloomy by constantly saying that profit margins will always go down, but that is the case with the majority of businesses unless if they're lucky and they can take advantage of some of the emerging technologies or the business owner is savvy enough of finding ways for saving costs at all times.

Some of the ways you can increase your profits are: reduce cost of goods, reduce advertising costs by finding more value for money solutions, increase price by giving a reasonable justification such as things like new improved formula, enhance your branding thereby charging more, becoming more efficient including becoming more tax efficient and getting rid of anything that is not being utilised but is weighing the business down such as extra staff.

YOUR DAILY TARGET

Any business that you start now or have been running for a while must have a single day target, this means the amount of money you need to turn over that day to remain in business and to reach your profit target.

This daily target will be a division of your yearly target and it is something that should pretty much be set in stone and should be adhered to but not at the cost of margin. Many people make the mistake of eating into their margins to try and hit their daily targets. This is a classic way of sinking your business when you try and do more turnover or maintain your current turnover at the cost of profit. It is a big no-no.

Reducing prices is a classic way of losing profit margin, something that is in fact in your control unlike rising costs. Whilst reducing prices may be a good strategy for the very short term, it is never a good practice for the long-term survival of your business.
The same goes for people who give freebies to try and increase business or starting a business with the introduction of free

products or free services. Imagine you're just starting out as a beauty therapist and you give free sessions, which is fine to get a few clients but if you continue to do that, then not only will your profit margin be zero but in fact you will be making a huge loss after a while because you're giving your time which costs you, for nothing.

Going back to my very early example of the bicycle, I will remind you that you must at all times keep your balance on the bike and balance is profit. Think of an introductory offer as a quick downhill to get you going; it can't take you on your road forever. There are many strategies for getting your business going and sometimes you may not make profit very early on which is okay as long as you have a strategy for catching up later and becoming profitable. In fact many businesses start off by not making a profit for many months or sometimes many years. To me they are very scary businesses and I have never been a fan of those, so I can only tell you about my own personal experiences and I would never do a business which is not profitable within a short period of time.

However I do understand that sometimes you have to give free products, free services or spend a great deal on branding and advertising before you see any returns. But this investing in your business and spending a lot before you receive any money should also be a big part of your business plan and you should be able to show it as part of your costs. Your business plan may very well show no profit or a loss in the early months but then because you would be recouping your initial investment, you start seeing a higher profit margin as time goes by.

Everything is in the planning, and if you cannot show that you would recoup your initial investment exactly and accurately then no one will invest in your business and if you are using your own savings you better be careful because if you cannot show to yourself that you are going to recoup your initial investment then you're in trouble. Many people hope or pray that something will happen or that they will get lucky and they will make money or see a return on their investment but they don't really have a plan for it and this is very wrong. You cannot hope to make money, you must plan to make money. If you cannot clearly show that your investment in every pound spent or in every hour of your services given free and every free product, is going to give you an exact amount back, then you are better off not doing it. I know that many people say it's good to speculate to accumulate but this is really a fool's game when there are so many tools at your disposal for an exact return.

HOW TO INCREASE TURNOVER

I do talk a lot about profit and this book is about having a profitable business however if you don't have any turnover and you don't have any money coming in then you won't have any profit either. So, how do you increase turnover? Once again it is all in the planning and the planning document that you have created at the outset of your business which will include your brand proposition, your advertising and marketing strategy, your full pricing and your goals for the first six months, year, five years and an eventual possible exit.

Turnover can be increased by advertising, marketing, recommendations, innovation, sales techniques such as cross selling or up-selling, mass distribution, expanding such as opening more shops or franchises or hiring more people. For most businesses, as turnover increases, profit margins come down and this is normal and to a certain extent you shouldn't worry about it, however you should have a red alert level and when your profit margin falls below that then you need to start looking at your whole business from costs to pricing and the speed of growth. You want to always keep your balance on the bicycle as you speed along; if you're speeding too much you will start to lose your balance i.e. affecting your profit.

You can hire someone to increase your turnover if you've reached a plateau and you can no longer do it yourself. There is no shame in that and you must never have pride or ego when it comes to growing your business and remaining profitable. I will address this point in other books because it is a huge subject but always remember that you are the person you should be relying on and whilst others can help you, you must never give your entire business to someone else hoping that they will grow it for you. You would be very lucky to find someone that will grow your business like that, without either wanting a huge amount of money which may eat into your profits or without stealing your business. I'm not saying that this person does not exist; I am just saying that they are very far and few and don't be sitting there relying on them to show up.

These days there are so many smart ways of increasing business turnover and the best piece of advice I can give you is once again going back to the mind and the power of your mind and your own aspirations. If you have it in mind to have a great business with a high turnover and big profit, then you will find ways of increasing the turnover. However if you are thinking small then chances are your mind will not search for ways of increasing your turnover. In every industry and in every business, and I promise you this, there is a way of increasing turnover if you choose to do so and if your mind is strong enough. There are so many ways of increasing turnover and the winners are those that don't sit still and don't look back at what has worked for them in the past necessarily because many times it is new technologies and new emerging marketing tools that can help you increase turnover.

Look at Facebook for example as a way of advertising. Facebook was seen not so long ago as a vehicle that cannot do anything for businesses who want to increase their turnover and Google was the king. Really, I remember this and it is interesting to see that Facebook has taken Google on and is actually doing a better job than Google because of all the information that Facebook has on people around the world which Google could only dream of. They even say Facebook has helped elections and for candidates to win. A huge proportion of the world's population is on Facebook and they have entered all their details into Facebook's database so if you are a smart business person and you tap into this huge database, you can pretty much target anyone and grow your business in any direction you wish; but of course you need to know how to use Facebook advertising. I'm telling you this to give you an example of an emerging way that businesses can increase turnover; something that was not around not so long ago.

At the end of the day if you are a survivor and if your mind is strong and if you have high ambitions you will always win. The problem arises when your mind is not strong enough or there are interferences with your mind and you start having a defeatist attitude to your business and that is when things will start going wrong.

You can only read so much and emulate so much; a lot of your business life will be spent trialling and finding your own feet such as sampling, giving free products, giving free time incentives, cutting prices, different marketing strategies and using social media in your own way and in your own industry.

YOU MUST GIVE VALUE

I may emphasise the point of making high profit a lot but never mistake it with being unethical. At the end of the day if you're giving a great value product or service to someone and they are happy to pay for it, there is nothing wrong with that. I will always advise you to have high integrity, high morals and never do anything illegal. When you give value to people, you can never go wrong and they will always recommend you and come back to you.

Some businesses do grow unethically and prosper and stay around for a long time, perhaps because there is no competition to them or they have been established for a long time, but as a general rule you must be ethical and you must give good value. You can give good value if you are selling cheap and you can still give good value if you're selling expensive but value is the perception of the customer that they are getting a good deal for the money they are spending. This perception comes along from a combination of things such as your marketing, your design/look/feel, your branding, your packaging, your customer services, your after sales and your follow-ups.

Recently I hired an office in London with one of the biggest office space companies in the world. During the time that I had my office, I had to deal with three or four different managers because they kept leaving the company which didn't seem very good to me at the time. The office was good and generally I was happy with their service although they had quite a lot of additions that I had to keep asking them to remove; things that I hadn't asked for such as tea or coffee or telephone or postal service. At first I found it quite annoying that they kept adding things to a bill which should have been a straightforward bill but I didn't think much of it because I was only having the office for a while.

Subsequently after leaving the office and handing my keys, I realised just what a terrible company they were because they kept billing me and re-billing me for things from postal redirection and phone service which I never used, to another month and another month, even though I was no longer there. The original manager that had dealt with was long gone and nobody seemed to know anything about my office and it became a legal issue for me to get back money which they kept charging on my credit card for an office I was no longer using. It was crazy, this company is absolutely huge and they have offices in many cities around the world and to have such a disgusting service was unbelievable. Needless to say I will never ever use them again even if I was desperate and I will never recommend them to anyone. In fact I have made sure that as many of my business friends know about just what a disreputable company they are. I have since found out that they have a terrible reputation and this is their strategy for dealing with people who use their services. This is very surprising to me because they are a very large company and I wouldn't have thought that they need to be so aggressive and so bad at customer services.

The above example is just to illustrate that when somebody gets value for money and they get a good deal, they will recommend that to others and on the flip side if you think you haven't got a good deal, you will tell as many of your friends as possible and in turn this will not be good for the company involved. It will sooner or later catch up with them. This is why I am saying always start an ethical company and have ethical practices and never do anything illegal or immoral and always try and do good for your customers no matter how large or small. I think as long as you do good and you stick to sound business and customer services practices, you cannot go wrong. You will always have people who may complain and may not agree with some of the things that you are doing but you are not there to please everybody. You are there to make a good amount of profit and give a good service or product to as many people as possible but remember nobody can please everybody out there so never be guided or re-routed according to complaints or the opinion of a few. You can get their opinion and try and better your product or services but you are not there to please people or be guided by the masses. They are there to buy your product or services based on the principles "you've" put in place; not the other way round!

HOW TO CHOOSE YOUR MARKET

Cheap and cheerful - are your customers or clientele going to be cheap and cheerful and buy your product or services at a low price and give you a relatively low margin? If this is your target audience then you need to have a very good think about your business before you embark on your journey through the muddy and often turbulent waters of business. The main problem with selling cheap and cheerful products or services is that anybody else can come in at your price or at a slightly lower price and can take your customers and your business away. When your business is extremely price sensitive and this is often the case with businesses that are in the lower end of the market, then you better be good at what you're doing otherwise your business is always at risk of being taken over by competitors and destroyed because someone else comes in at a lower price than you.

Luxury and high-end - on the opposite direction to cheap and cheerful is luxury and high-end and this is where you can charge the highest prices and make the most margins and personally this is where I prefer to be and this is where I recommend people who are just starting out a new business to start. I am more comfortable advising you on how to make maximum profit and keep high margins and I have seen that businesses which have a good profit margin tend to fare better especially if there is a downturn in the economy which is what's been happening over the last few years and at the time of writing this book.

There is no right and wrong here and it really all depends on the product and service that you are marketing. For example you could sell a very cheap product with very little margin but it is new and innovative and nobody else has it and you are unlikely to have competition for long while to come, in which case you're home free for many years making profit and not having any competitors interfere with your business. Your geographical location could have a bearing on whether you should start a low or high end business and whether you will have competition or interference with your business. This is why I say that nobody can tell you what to do. You can get advice from people and you can read and listen to them but at the end of the day they don't live where you live, they don't know what you know, they don't have your skills or lack of skills and they don't know what your drive is like. They are not inside your head!

Lots of people make it in the low sectors of the economy and lots of people make it with high-end products and services but the principle factor remains which is, whichever business you are in, if you are not profitable, your business will not last for very long and it will eventually go under.

As long as you are sticking to daily targets and weekly targets and monthly targets and you are not falling too far behind, you will be okay. You should start worrying if your turnover is going down and your costs are going up and you are finding it difficult to pay people on time. There are always warning signs in business but most often business people don't see them or they think they can fix them and whilst some of them are fixable, some of them are not. Bear in mind that a big warning sign that you may be in trouble is if you are not able to pay people on time, whether it is your staff or any supplier or anyone that invoices you and you have to deal with on a regular basis.

I am not going to kid you and tell you that business is easy or that you will be successful, because the odds are stacked against you and statistically most businesses fail. But in reality that really doesn't mean much because most businesses just get started by the principal without any necessary planning, advice, goal setting, marketing, advertising, branding or paying attention to principles such as the ones being mentioned in this book. In a way you are ahead of the game because you have actually bothered to show that you're serious and are reading about business and how to start and be profitable, so you definitely have a head-start on 99% of other people that go into business. As I write this, I sincerely hope that you will become successful in business and I would be very happy to know that I have been a small part of someone's successful business journey.

HOW TO DO YOUR OWN MARKETING

You've heard the saying horses for courses and I really believe this saying in business. Something that may work for one person or one company may not work for you at all and this is why I say you have to follow your own journey and not worry too much about others. It is good to be aware of lots and lots of ways to market your business but you mustn't assume that a particular marketing method that is working for someone else will work for you. The only time you can rely on someone else's marketing methods for your own business is if that business is identical to yours and if you have inside knowledge as to exactly what marketing tools they are using and that you know it is working very well for them.

Otherwise you have to use your own knowledge which you can gain from reading. There are lots of places to currently promote your business: Facebook, Instagram, Twitter, SoundCloud, podcasts, blogs, Snapchat, Pinterest, YouTube, Google and lots and lots of online places where you can advertise. There are also lots of other companies that do things like abandoned basket takeovers, follow-me ads, and newer technologies involving seriously pinpointing the exact customer that will be perfect for your business.

I will give you a bit of advice especially when you're first starting out, and that is if you can, spend no money at all, as long as you can get business in. The best way of starting your business is actually spending no money at all and trying to grow it organically. Then when you have some money coming in you can start spending a little bit and testing the marketing waters and seeing what works for you. Only fools start spending and spending on lots of different marketing ideas without any concrete proof that there will be a return. The exception is if a company or a person has previous experience with those marketing methods for that same industry and is 100% certain that they will give results. I have seen it so many times when people just go crazy with their marketing without actually seeing a return or knowing what they are doing.

A friend of a friend of mine opened a sandwich shop in one of the arcades in East London many years ago. He spent a lot of money on branding and on the look and feel of the shop and quite a lot on marketing and for a while he was doing very well but he pretty much used up all his budget on marketing and had no more money left to even buy stock. The shame of it is that he probably would have succeeded had he just opened up with a few customers and let his business grow organically especially because it was in a very good location by itself. Spending unnecessary money on marketing and advertising ended up being his downfall because he used all of his cashflow which should have been used for more essential things such as staff wages and buying the ingredients for his foods.

One of the most important things with marketing is that you must track everything; spending a bit of time on numbers and being good at maths helps you in business and if you don't start with this habit of tracking everything then you may get in trouble later on along the way. In fact one of the best habits a businessperson can develop is to look at statistics and to track all their marketing and advertising. If you spend 10p and got back 20p and you have attracted customers and sales, then you're in a good place; however if you spent 10p and you have no idea whether it is giving you 20p or nothing then you are not on to a good start.

When I started one of my earliest businesses I took out one advert in one magazine which I knew would give me good returns. I negotiated a very good rate with that magazine and I made sure that I had very good copy and a powerful message and image in the advert. The advert was on the right-hand page early on in the magazine and I made sure it was as powerful as it could be. I tracked the returns from that advert and only took out a second page when the first page was clearly paying for itself. I took out more pages in more magazines ensuring that each and every page would be paying for itself.

The same was done for Google advertising as well when I started one of my first businesses. I made sure that every campaign was giving a good return and everything was tracked so the overall spend on the campaign was never ever more than the return from the campaign. Depending on your profit margin you can decide how much you can spend on advertising. For example if your product is selling for £50 and the cost of your product is 5 pounds then you can easily afford 50p or £1 to acquire a customer. Assuming your other costs are not very high you may even be able to go up to £10 to acquire a new customer but it is important for you to track the exact cost of acquiring each and every new customer. Basically it is important for you to track everything in your business and that is why even if you give your business to someone else to run, you must always be on top of it and be aware of costs and returns.

Many things that I am telling you in this book are my own personal experiences and I have been very successful with these principles and am sharing them with you to ensure that you are successful too, so please bear in mind that I am not telling you pie in the sky theories, I am telling you real life proven and tested principles of sound business. Things like tracking your advertising spend and the revenue it's giving you is worth its weight in gold. In addition to ensuring that you are tracking your advertising spend and revenues from it, you must also be open to any other advertising mediums but I would really stress not to be taken in with cold-callers telling you how wonderful their advertising medium is, because if it was so wonderful they wouldn't have to call you about it and you would have probably heard about it already.

Some of the most successful companies in the world especially these days, have amazing tracking technologies and they track revenues, they track recommendations, they track coupons, they track discount codes, and they make sure that each penny they spend is justified. I opened a shop a few years ago and we put in this screen in the back of the shop which was interactive. This screen was so amazing in that it could tell if a man or a woman was standing in front of it. Without the customer knowing, the screen would show a relevant advert according to the sex of the customer standing in front of it. The world has changed so much and technology is improving at such a rapid pace that you must embrace all new technologies that can help you gain new customers, keep new customers and ensure they are loyal to your brand and spread the word about your brand.

In each industry there is a number of secret promotional, marketing, and advertising methods that can promote your business. It is your job to find those and to stay away from the others which will give you no returns. Just because you have heard of a magazine does not mean that it is a good magazine or that it will give you great returns. Just because you have not heard of a method for marketing your business, does not mean that it may not be useful to you. I do think though that you should definitely stay away from those who cold-call you and try and sell you something when you are not prepared for it.

There are some lucky people in this world, and I say luck because in some way they are lucky but in other ways they have created their own luck; they have a business that grows without much being spent on advertising or marketing. They have amazing products or services that just get recommended and they very rarely have to advertise. Recently there was a personal trainer with a new book that was one of Amazon's all-time bestsellers and you know what? The book wasn't coming out for another six months and it was a best-seller on Amazon! This person had done an incredible job on social media of selling their brand and selling the business and ultimately selling the book. This is the beauty of the age we live in, and that you really just need a phone, determination, a good idea, set plan and lots of perseverance to make money. Lots of people are doing this, making a lot of money from their phones without much else.

I really and truly believe that there has never been a better time to start your own profitable business than right now. Technology has enabled us to be able to make money like never before. Take the example of a person that reposts other people's pictures under a specific theme such as cars, travel, luxury and so on. This person can grow on Instagram, have a good following and charge people for advertising on their page. In effect they just make money out of the phone and being smart enough to choose the right photos, tag them in the right way and create a page which is interesting to advertisers. There are very many of these opportunities in today's technologically advanced world and this is why I say you live in a world full of opportunity, if you are serious enough, determined enough and have a good idea with passion to see it through.

THE POWER OF RECOMMENDATION

Some of the biggest companies in the world have started out small but harnessed the power of recommendation and have been very aware of the advantages of getting each and every customer to recommend their product or services to others. Many young business people start off thinking that they have to spend money and they have to advertise and for some reason have the belief that in order to get revenues to come in, you have to spend on outside mediums.

Whilst it is true that one has to spend money in order to grow one's brand, one must not underestimate the power of recommendation. Recommendations come in all shapes and forms from the simple recommend a friend scheme to MLN, pyramid schemes, loyalty and reward schemes. One of my biggest competitors in one of my businesses in fact started in his garage and grew his business to a multi-million pound turnover business by harnessing the power of recommendations. He used in some ways a very sophisticated, yet simple way of getting customers to recommend others by using a code that they were given once they signed up or bought a product from him. The more people you would give the code out to, the more rewards you would get from his company. He basically incentivised each and every customer to go out there and become his salesman. What better way than getting your own customers to do your donkey work and creating a win-win situation where the customer is rewarded for recommending others, who would then go on and recommend others and your business grows and grows as a result of a very clever recommendation scheme.

Another example I can give you goes back some 30 years to a company called Galaxy sales who used to sell rotating satellite dishes. The dish would cost you something like £3000, however if you recommended six other people, the dish would cost you nothing. Galaxy sales also used this clever system of growing their business, although these days some would call this an unethical way of doing business.

Obviously you should not do anything which is illegal or immoral as a foundation for your business because at some stage it will catch up with you and can do more harm than all the good that you've done over many years. However, you should definitely consider putting in place a strong, rewarding, and active recommendation scheme in whatever business you are running. As you can see it is a win-win in that you get each and every customer to bring you more customers and more revenues, and customers benefit by recommending your brand to the people they know. In fact in the first example I gave above, customers would very often use the code and plaster it all over the place recommending the brand to more people that they didn't even know. How beautiful is this scheme where you get your customers to recommend your brand to friends, colleagues and anyone and everyone that they come across or not come across?

BUSINESS SIMPLIFIED

So on a very simple level business is:

Idea —> Research —> Planning —> Starting —> Marketing —> Tracking —> Doing more of What Works —> Hitting Targets —> Growth —> More Innovation —> Possibly an Exit.

People should see business as a simple flowchart and as long as you don't deviate from this flowchart you should have success.

STARTING OUT

Let's talk a bit more about this subject because it is one that seems to be an important one to would be entrepreneurs. I receive many messages asking how they can start a business or how they can get the funds to start a business. Often people complicate matters more than it need be. The basic rule is that if your business idea is good, chances are you will sooner or later get off the ground with it if you're persistent enough. Getting funds is difficult but it is as difficult as the effort you put in to get those funds. Do not underestimate the power of relatives, friends or investors, all too happy to invest in you if you can show them that your idea is viable, that you are hard-working, and that they will get a good return on their investment.

One of the biggest mistakes you can make is to start out too big and try and compete with people that have been in business for a very long time. Some people do this, but this is not necessarily the right way and the competitors may have just got lucky. You cannot emulate other people because you do not know their circumstances. You have to use logic and the basic sound principles of business to ensure short-term and long-term success.

As well as getting help from the people around you in terms of financial help, you can of course get them to help you physically as well in those early stages. Your wife, husband, brother, sister, mother, father, children or friends can all help you in their spare time and the majority may not even want payment for their efforts because they will be all too happy to help you start on your new venture.

If you can do everything yourself, you should do so in those early days. Many people will tell you to delegate and not use your precious time for doing stuff, however I totally disagree with this. When you're first starting out, you need to understand every aspect of your business and therefore you need to get your hands dirty and truly understand your business from the ground up. You will not understand how your business runs or operates properly if you start hiring people to do most of the work. Never mind the fact that precious profit is going to be given away or wasted on employees and staff when it need not be.

In order to have a profitable business short-term and long-term, the simple fact is that you need to be profitable and it is very difficult to be profitable when you start spending all your money and raising your costs. I can tell you from my own personal experience that when I first started my first business, I did everything myself. I was their marketing manager, general manager, Internet guru, packer, advertising manager, export manager, wholesale manager, customer services manager, customer services agent, designer, shop assistant and pretty much everything else that needed doing. I was exhausted and tired most days but full of drive and determination and extremely happy to not be paying people to do jobs that I could do myself and saving costs, thereby making sure I was profitable pretty much from the very first week of trading.

I realise that every business is different, but you get the idea. If you can save costs you must save costs. I come across so many people that just don't understand this simple principle of business which is only hire if you really really have to - and even then, think twice!

In fact it's funny but going back a few years when my turnover was equal to one of my main competitors in one of my businesses, I had five people working for me and he had 55 people working for him and our turnovers were identical! How do you explain that? Some people just get into the habit of hiring more and more people and sometimes hiring people to help those who don't do the job very well or those that mess up their jobs. My advice to you is to save save save and make sure you are profitable and only hire when you absolutely have to.

One of the earliest businesses I started was an import export business with a friend of mine. I remember my friend wanted to buy everything brand-new; he wanted a new fax machine, new phones, new printer and so on. I decided to stop working with him immediately because to me, he just didn't understand business and didn't understand saving costs to ensure maximum profitability. Surprise surprise, 25 years on I am driving in the latest hypercar and he is still driving in an old banged-up van. It just goes to show that some people do not understand the basic fundamentals of business even when you explain it to them in clear terms.

On the same principles discussed above, if you can rent, then you must rent rather than buying. If you can get out of committing to something, then you mustn't commit to it until you are very profitable. By this I mean things like long-term contracts with telecommunications companies or anything that will tie you down and cost you a lot of money without you knowing exactly where you are going in those early stages.

Not spending unnecessary money is a very important principle in business especially when you're first starting out. This principle is obviously valid throughout your business life and many people once they start making some money, they start spending unnecessary amounts and forgetting how and where they started out from which is a shame because they probably can remain more profitable if they stick to the founding principles of their business, one of which is minimum spend for maximum profits.

Spend is not just counting staff or equipment, spending unnecessarily can also include things like taking out patents and trademarks and spending money on intellectual property where you need not. The goal is always minimum spend, maximum return.

I had a friend of mine who had a number of properties across London and in the 10 years that I knew him, he had not spent a penny on renovating any of the properties and he was earning quite a lot of money from each property. I also know other property developers and property owners who spent a large amount of their revenue every year to upgrade and refurbish their properties, somewhat unnecessarily and thereby eating into their profits. Obviously everyone is different and every entrepreneur will do things their own way, but I hope you can be more like my friend who did not spend unnecessarily than other people who believed they needed to constantly spend money that they could have otherwise saved and increase their profits.

THE IMPORTANCE OF PERSISTENCE AND NOT GIVING UP

Once you have an idea and you have a goal and you have a plan, the most important thing for you to remember is to stick to your plan. You must never give up and you must see your entrepreneurial journey as a long journey of many ups and many downs and many failures and many successes. The problem with most people is that they give up, many people give up at the outset as soon as they hit one obstacle and others give up a little bit further along the way. In the mind of the person that gives up, they have valid justifications for why they are giving up. However if you speak to any successful business person or successful person for that matter, you will see that failure or giving up was never an option for them at any stage; whether early on or later on, because giving up was never an option, the only option they had was to find a solution.

This is a very important concept to understand when it comes to your mind and the power of your mind; when giving up is even a slight option in your mind then you leave the door open to doubt and you give yourself the option of giving up. However when giving up is absolutely not an option and does not exist in your business plan in any shape or form, then your mind does something very interesting in that it tries to find solutions to your problems. The mind is very adept and always ready to find solutions to the biggest problems that you may face in business, however if you are not minded (pardon the pun!) to find solutions, then chances are you will fail at some stage.

IF YOU ARE NOT GROWING, YOU ARE SHRINKING AND THE IMPORTANCE OF GROWING SLOWLY

If you don't understand the concept of profit from very early on, then you are very unlikely to understand it later on because you wouldn't have trained yourself properly in business and in being profitable. This is why if you get a small profit early on in your business life, this is worth it's weight in gold because that experience of knowing how to make a profit is extremely valuable. Many times you will see people tell you that they have lost everything but they don't care because they have experience and they can use their experience to build their business up again. You must understand that if you manage to make a profit in any endeavour, then you are way ahead of 90% of other people that do business because that 90% either do not make a profit or stop making a profit after a very short time.

If you can grow slowly and you can get yourself in a position where you have made a small profit early on and you build on that profit and make a bigger profit as your business progresses, then as long as you are sticking to the sound principles highlighted in this book, there is no reason why you cannot continue to be profitable and to have a business with longevity.

There is nothing wrong with having a business which is lean and making profit, there's nothing wrong with hiring someone only when you need to and only when that person is going to pay for themselves, there is nothing wrong with not having prestigious offices when you first start out. There is nothing wrong with not having a Ferrari or Lamborghini in the first few years of your business because you are not making the money of some of the other people that you see. I would say especially more so these days with social media, many of the people that you see supposedly making great profits in their businesses are actually not very successful at all. Once again I emphasise the point that you must only be concerned with your own business and not with how others are doing or what supercar they are driving.

As you slowly grow and make a profit and you follow your plan for growth, you will be going towards a bigger path and making more money, however not at the expense of profits. The saying that you are either shrinking or growing is extremely true when it comes to business and business life. Nothing is truer in business than the very fact that you must always concentrate on growth and must never let lack of growth catch you off guard.

WHAT YOU SHOULD SPEND YOUR MONEY ON IN THE EARLY STAGES OF YOUR BUSINESS AND HOW NOT TO LOSE IT ALL

We've talked extensively about saving money and not spending unnecessary money on things that will eat into your profit in the early stages of business and as your business continues to grow. The question now is what should you spend money on because just as you will not make profits by spending unnecessarily, chances are that you will not grow or make any profits if you are not spending any money especially on the things you should be spending money on.

Clearly if you spent 10p and you got back £10, then that is a good amount of return and that is something that you should probably spend money on. Anything that brings you a high turnover and great profits is worth spending your money on. Here, "opportunity cost" comes into effect and this is where advertising rather than staff that you may not need and will not bring you any extra revenue, may be a better spend. It is clearly better to spend £30,000 on advertising that may potentially give you £200,000 than spending £30,000 on a member of staff whose job you could do yourself. This is once again where statistics and numbers come into play and why you must always be on top of numbers when it comes to your business. For example if you have £10,000 extra to spend on growing your business, you should clearly spend it on advertising and marketing that you know statistically will bring you more revenues than a piece of machinery or spending on a member of staff. When I say statistically and "you know", I mean that you have tested the returns out on a small scale and you know what you spend will give you good returns. Smart business people always track everything as mentioned earlier and smart business people do not listen to other people's opinions but go with their own gut instinct and spend their money wisely when it comes to growing their business and scaling up.

Another important tip for you to remember is that costs are not necessarily what you see them to be at first. By that I mean every cost given to you can be negotiated down. Sometimes you may even come across a cost that in your mind you cannot negotiate down such as the cost of telecommunications from a large provider; however I will disagree with anyone that believes this and I will tell you that if you want and have the desire, you can get a cheaper cost on everything including things that may be set in their price.

In my own business life especially early on, I negotiated every cost to be lower and lower and continued to do so well into the 10th year of my business life. However as you grow bigger and you have much more turnover and more important things, sometimes you forget the importance of negotiating costs down which is a very important thing to never forget!

Much like a Moroccan souk or bazaar where you expect prices to be negotiable, I would argue that your road to business success which is paved with many costs and many suppliers can also be negotiated along the way. I cannot remember anything that I did not negotiate down from cost of products, wage expectations by staff, cost of transport, cost of packaging, cost of telecommunications, stationary and anything and everything to do with business.

You need to be smart and tell people that you're going to be doing great business with them and lots and lots of volume to get their juices flowing to deal with you and give you the best prices. Usually when you get those early best prices, companies will not put your prices up at a later stage because they value your business and don't want to lose your business. This is an important tip to remember.

Another assumption that people make, is that whatever prices they have been given cannot be negotiated again at some time in the future, which is totally wrong. Depending on where you are in your business, your negotiation skills, your volumes and how badly you want it, you can always negotiate prices with suppliers at any given time. The old adage of if you don't ask, you don't get is very much operational in this field of business.

Now, there is a trap which you mustn't fall into which is constantly asking for lower prices. If you were minded to do this all the time, then you may find that your suppliers will give you much higher prices, factoring in the fact that you keep asking for reduced prices! This is not a good position to be in because you never know the real price of the goods you will be getting because your suppliers have lost faith and trust in you and see you as someone that constantly requires multiple discounts.

In business life much like life itself you must walk with your head up high and looking ahead of you. This means you must look to increase revenues, grow bigger and go further. Whilst it is important to reduce costs and look down every once in awhile, it is important to look ahead and look up and look at the bigger picture. The billionaires and multimillionaires that you see, think this way, they always think of the bigger picture and whilst they are good negotiators when it comes to costs, they tend to concentrate more on increasing revenues and profits.

Negotiation is a skill, if you do not already possess this extremely valuable tool, this book does not have the scope to deal with negotiation skills as that is a whole new topic in itself. However, being able to negotiate and being aware that negotiating prices down whilst running a profitable business should be at the forefront of your mind at all times.

SOME SECRET RULES OF BUSINESS AND HOW YOU CAN STAY PROFITABLE WITHOUT RISKING LOSING YOUR BUSINESS

HONESTY

This may be an obvious thing, however honesty is extremely important when it comes to running a business or brand, supplying products or services. Some people even start off being honest and wanting to do good, but somewhere along the line, probably when they stop being profitable, they forget this very important principle of business. In fact one of the foundations of any good business, or any relationship for that matter is honesty.

Honesty is giving people what you believe to be true and what you believe is what you have set out to offer and whether it is a product or service, what you believe they are paying money for and are expecting to receive. I go back to the earlier point of you needing to be in a business which is legal and moral.

GIVING VALUE

A customer of your business must believe that they are receiving value when it comes to using your products or services. It doesn't matter if they pay one dollar for your product or $10000. Value is what they perceive they have received in exchange for the money given to you. Any customer that does not believe they have received value from you, albeit at any price will not recommend your products, will not become a loyal customer and will not be a long-term prospect for your business.

Many people start off giving value to customers, however somewhere along the line they lose track of this very important business principle. For example, let's say you are a physiotherapist and you charge £50 for one hour's worth of physiotherapy. Your clients are happy and your customer base starts to grow. After a while you find that you cannot take on any more clients because your time is fully booked and you are tired by the end of the day. So, you start charging the same amount but giving 50 minutes of physiotherapy rather than a full hour. At first this may be going well until you start to lose customers because they no longer perceive to be receiving value for money.

Recently a very well-known chocolate manufacturer decided to reduce the size of their world-famous chocolate ever so slightly for probably economical reasons. The result was chaos, complaints and loss of sales. Their excuse, albeit a pathetic one, was that customers had requested this new smaller size. Clearly this is not true and for them it was all about making the additional profit and as you may have guessed the price of the new smaller bar was exactly the same as the old larger bar. Therefore the customer no longer perceived that they were getting value for money, which is very subjective in many ways.

GIVING GOOD SERVICE

You will never go wrong if you are in the service industry and you give exceptional service to customers. The same principle applies if you are selling a product and give amazing service prior to purchase, during purchase and after sales. Especially more important in today's world, giving exceptional service, will make you stand out from the rest of the crowd. There are lots of different business models and many people don't give great service and they get away with it, which is fine if it works for them. However the principles laid down in this book are the essential principles of business in my opinion and I would never put not giving great service or not worrying about how you come across to the customer, as a great way of doing business.

Many people may decide that too much time, effort and money is spent on giving good service and they may have a product or service that is not worthy of the extra spend on "great service". I do not think this is a sound principle of business. Let's put it another way, if things go wrong for you in business and you start losing profits or turnover, if you've been giving great service along the way, at least you can take that off the list of possible causes for your downfall.

BE AS GOOD AS YOUR WORD

I remember when I first started my very first business, if I told someone I would call them back within five minutes, I made sure I called them back within three. Some people don't value integrity that much, and for them, this works in the short term and if they're lucky in the long term. However not having integrity and not being as good as your word is not a good start or good way to conduct your business.

I strongly urge you to adopt good principles such as having high integrity when it comes to dealing with everyone including staff, suppliers, adversaries and anyone else that you may come across in your business life. Personally, I would say the things that are very important to me as a result of my business life, one is the experience I have gained, the other is the reputation that I have built as being a person of integrity with very high standards. This does not mean that I am nice to everybody; to the contrary I am not very nice to the people that are not nice to me, however if I promise you something and I tell you I will do something, I will 100% do it. To me, this is having integrity and it is very useful in business.

For example, sometimes I have been sent millions of pounds worth of stock without paying for it upfront. I have been given this amazing line of credit because the owners of those companies know that I am a man of principle and they can trust me. I know it sounds strange for you to think about business like this, however business is a relationship at the end of the day. Be it a relationship with your customers or your suppliers and if you are a person of integrity and they can see that, then this will open doors for you and ensure that you have good relationships with those that you need to.

If I tell you I am going to sue you, I am 100% going to sue you and you can expect a letter within normally a couple of days! At the same token, if I tell you I am going to pay you by Friday, then you can be assured I will pay you by Friday. I call this integrity and being a person of principle and I would advise you to adopt a similar strategy in your business even if you think you can get away with not having integrity.

At this point you may be asking what does being honest, having integrity, or giving amazing service has to do with being very profitable? I say everything. A sound business needs sound foundations and the things that we are talking about in this section are sound foundations for any business and also any relationship. Whilst many people get away with not being honest or having integrity in their personal relationships, you will find that these values go a long way in relationships that matter to you especially if your partner in business is on the same wavelength as you. In other words, if in business you are also dealing with people of high integrity and high values, then you will be rewarded for your high principles.

PAY ATTENTION TO QUALITY

Many businesses start off with good intentions giving products with great quality and they attract new customers and the business grows. Many other businesses start getting into trouble and quality starts to suffer as a result of this and this is where owners look to cut corners which may benefit them in the short run but rarely does cutting corners benefit in the long run for most businesses.

I will give you an example from one of my own businesses which is a sports nutrition business selling high-quality supplements. Whey protein is a by-product of milk and cheese manufacturing and sports nutrition companies sell whey protein to their customers for the development of their muscles. When the industry first started, whey protein was relatively cheap and the profits were high. After a while whey prices started to go higher and higher and so protein companies compromised and reduced the quality and mixed their whey protein with other cheaper protein sources.

I do not believe in reducing the quality of a product for higher profits or maintenance of current profits and therefore my company was probably the only one in the sports nutrition sector that did not compromise the quality of its whey protein. Did sales get affected? Of course they did and I probably lost some customers because the price point was high for a high quality product, however the keyword here is quality and in the long run the business did not really get affected because those customers that valued real quality and did not want their brand to compromise on quality due to supply and pricing issues, stayed with my brand.

There is a lesson to be learned here, which is if you know your customer and you know that they value quality and that is the reason why they buy from you, whether it is services or goods that you are selling, then maintaining the high quality of your product is probably a good idea.

You see, once you reduce the quality of your product and you get to be known in the industry as having compromised the quality of your product, then it may be very difficult to get back that reputation of being a brand with high quality. There have been many brands throughout the world that have reduced the quality of their products and as a result have suffered in reputation, sales and ultimately profitability. Some very well known high street brands that were known for quality and being high end, have ended up in multiple discount stores and being regarded as a low quality discount brand because they compromised on the quality of their products.

THE IMPORTANCE OF GIVING A GUARANTEE

If you really believe in your product or service, you may want to consider giving a guarantee to your customer. I know what you're thinking, that you will lose lots of business and it is not a good idea to leave the doors open for customers to bring back products or ask for their money back. If you manage to get everything else in your business right, offering a guarantee is often a great way of increasing revenue, increasing customer retention and loyalty and getting customers to recommend you to others.

In the businesses that I run, I always give a guarantee to the customer. Because at the end of the day you are not there to rip the customer off or take their money without giving them any assurance. I totally understand if you think that many customers will take advantage of your guarantee unfairly and it may cost you a lot. In my experience any guarantee outweighs the potential downfalls of not giving one or people wanting their money back. In fact in most of my businesses the percentage of returns is so small that it's not even worth mentioning. I am generalising here of course, I am sure there are industries where an unconditional guarantee can open the floodgates to lots of returns and a potential loss in profit or even bankruptcy. But on the whole giving a guarantee to the customer, especially an unconditional guarantee will reinforce your brand's integrity and will mean that customers will trust you more. This is especially more so for industries where customers are sceptical and need an additional assurance to make that final purchase; such as weight loss, giving advice, or anything new and innovative where the customer has no experience of that product or service.

Think of it as a relationship. Any relationship that starts off on sound foundations with both parties being honest, not lying, doing the best that they can, being open and trusting one another, can only be good. You can believe in karma or not and you can believe in high principles or not, at the end of the day it's your business. I know many business people that don't follow the principles of integrity, high moral values and giving customers great quality and great service and they succeed and you may also be one of them. But I cannot tell you if you will be lucky and it is better for you to be safe and follow sound principles rather than those of a few that get away with certain things.

EXAMPLES OF BUSINESSES THAT I CONSIDER TO BE GOOD

LOUIS VUITTON

I love the brand Louis Vuitton. Like them or hate them, they get so many things right. They have beautiful amazing stores that make you feel special when you walk in. They have very attentive and loyal and informed staff in all of their stores. They have great products with very high quality and the high quality is very consistent. Their packaging is absolutely amazing and makes you feel special when you purchase something from them. They have a great guarantee and returns policy and they give you the reassurance that when you spend money on their products, if you are not happy with your purchase then you are not stuck with that product. And if there is a fault, they rectify it promptly.

They are one of the world's most copied brands, and many times they have queues outside their stores for people waiting to get in to buy their products. How beautiful is that? Imagine having a brand where people queue up to purchase your product and they do not question your product and your prices at all and imagine not having to do discount sales when most of your competitors have to reduce their prices at some stage.

Louis Vuitton, to me is a brand that gets everything right and continues to innovate and keep customers coming back for more. They have got everything so perfect from their logo, look and feel, advertising, associations with celebrities, and the aforementioned packaging and stores. Even their website is innovative and no doubt takes a huge number of orders worldwide every day.

A GREAT HOTEL

I don't want to mention names because there are lots of different hotels that give amazing service and are worthy of a mention here. However I will give you an example of a hotel I stayed at in Egypt many years ago which to this day I tell other people about and recommend that they visit this particular hotel. The hotel had such welcoming staff that you would be forgiven to think they had shares in the hotel. Everything was timed to perfection from the greeting to fresh beverages upon arrival and just the way they came across from the very first moment you stepped in the hotel.

Nothing was too much to ask and everything was made to be perfect during your stay in this particular hotel. There are many hotels that are as good as this particular one, however they had so many things well thought of and effort was put into so many areas of their hospitality that I could not find anything to fault. In other words they had paid attention to all the things I have mentioned here which include quality of service, integrity, being true to their word and providing something over and above the competition; something that cannot be surpassed with ease.

LHW

Speaking of hotels, I want to talk about the Leading Hotels of the World (LHW) which is an umbrella brand operating the booking of a number of high end hotels around the globe. LHW have got service and standards and the expectations of customers perfectly right. When you book a room through the Leading Hotels of the World you are certain that you are going to get a very high level experience from their greeting upon arrival, to the cleanliness of the room, to the decor, to the room service, the common areas, courtesy of staff, friendliness and just about everything to do with a five star very high end experience.

There are of course many more exclusive hotels around the world and many websites which take bookings for hotels. However LHW only take on very specific hotels under their umbrella. In my experience they have set an extremely high standard for the hotels which fall under their group and can be booked through their website.

PAYING ATTENTION TO DETAIL

Paying attention to detail pays off in whatever service or product you are offering. Let's examine some areas where you can pay attention to detail and make sure that your business is profitable from the first day:

Packaging: the way you package your goods or your services is extremely important to how they are perceived. If you are a personal trainer, the way you do your hairstyle, the way your muscles are showing, your tan, your clothes and the way you have packaged yourself are extremely important in your business. The same goes for your products; if your product has great packaging, great branding, and arrives in the hands of the customer in the state that speaks quality and attention to detail, then you cannot go wrong.

I recently came across a sushi delivery business, much like hundreds of other sushi delivery businesses that exist these days. However this sushi delivery business had paid such close attention to their packaging, the colours they had chosen for the packaging and everything was packaged in their own packaging and everything was packed to perfection. You experienced their "brand" from start to finish.

How you are perceived is how your business really is, because if you think you have a great business but you don't pay attention to the most important aspects such as packaging, then how you are coming across to others is not the same as how you perceive your business to be. This is why surveys and market research is very important not just at the beginning of your business but throughout your business to see how your business is coming across to others.

Instructions: depending on what you are selling or what services you are giving, paying attention to instructions is extremely important. Going back to the example of a personal trainer, if you are a personal trainer that knows what they're talking about and communicate that effectively to potential customers, then you will have an advantage over others in the field.

The same goes if you are selling a product, if your instructions are comprehensive and well thought through and they give added value and simplicity to the customer, then this is a smart move on your part. Never neglect the importance of giving proper instructions for your goods or services to your ultimate end user.

Being courteous and answering people promptly: I usually spend a great deal of time and effort training staff to make sure they come across well and polite and caring and friendly. Whether you have a one-man business giving a service or a one-man business giving a product or you have a big business with many staff, it is important to provide a very high level of service.

Examples of these are simple things such as saying good afternoon or good morning instead of hello, not putting people on hold for too long without getting back to them, answering the phone straightaway, knowing what you're talking about and being well-informed on the product or services you are selling, being friendly and helpful and facilitating a scenario where people leave the conversation and you or your business has made a great impression on them. I cannot tell you the amount of times I have been impressed by salespeople in certain high-end stores or hotels. The extensive training that they get for high-end clients is something that does make a difference.

Knowledge: if you have more knowledge than your competitors and you have more certainty in what you are saying, then you will win that customer time and again. People are always looking for leaders and for businesses that are an authority in what they do. I cannot emphasise enough the importance of knowledge and why you must try and make yourself an authority in whatever it is that you are doing, be it providing services or products. If you're providing products then you must know your products extremely well inside and out. If you're providing services then you must know your competitors and all the ins and outs of what you are offering. It is also important to keep up-to-date with knowledge relevant to your industry and your business.

We human beings know when we are being taken for a ride and although sometimes we may not click, most definitely we will not go back to a provider of a service or a product that was not knowledgeable enough, high quality enough or gave the service and value that we expected.

Why do you think companies spend huge amounts on training their staff to have the maximum amount of knowledge? In fact if you have started a business or are about to start a business, I bet you are very knowledgeable in the field that you are going to get into, or I bet you are going to spend a great deal of time learning about that field. It is important to carry on with this search for knowledge and ensuring that you have the highest level of knowledge throughout your business life to ensure you remain as profitable as possible.

Being knowledgeable goes hand-in-hand with being profitable. And you may find that if your knowledge gets reduced, your profits are reduced.

Cleanliness: cleanliness goes all the way to the clean look of your premises and also applies to your own personal appearance or that of your team members or staff. It does not hurt to be clean, presentable and pristine.

Some companies, to their benefit, pay particular attention to the clean look of their brand, encompassing everything the customer experiences with their brand. Ultimately a brand, is a reflection of the person or people running their brand so if you are a messy person, you may not understand what I'm talking about here, however you must make an effort to present a clean brand and a clean business to your customers.

Greeting: we've already touched on greeting and how you should answer the phone to your customers, however by greeting I mean everything to do with how you come across to a customer upon first meeting you. Smiling is often a free and effective way of presenting yourself in a good light. If your business is not face-to-face, you can create a happy website or a happy advert or a happy-looking brand. Nobody wants a depressing brand or unhappy people. In fact there's nothing worse than dealing with a company and having to deal with rude or unhappy people.

Please pay particular attention to your greeting to your customer. If you can use the first name and be friendly with them, then please do so; this applies to emails and personal meetings.

Keeping standards: if you are lucky enough to have customers that are loyal to you and return to your business, then it is very important to keep the same standards that you have kept in the past. By this I mean people get used to a certain way of things being done and sometimes if you deviate from that, you may lose customers and profitability. For example there is a restaurant near me in Gibraltar, that has very good food and they always have the same meal with the same flavour in the same dish, provided in approximately 15 minutes, presented in the same way, and pretty much keep to the same standard time and again.

I can tell you for a fact that if I were to visit this restaurant and receive a different presentation, portion, flavour or anything different from what have been used to, then I may not go back there again. This does not stop you from providing a better service and a better standard to people, however the point I'm trying to make at this stage of the book is that in order to be successful and ultimately profitable you must not change the standard of your offering especially if you're looking for returning customers. Giving more is OK but giving less is a big no-no.

I can give you hundreds of examples of standards and how it is important to keep to those. For example if you were to buy a pair of shoes from Prada, you are going to get a box and some shoe bags with your shoes. You can choose not to take the box or not to take the shoe bags but as a regular customer of the brand, you will be expecting the shoe bags and the shoebox. If for any reason you did not receive the shoe bags, then you may question your purchase and it would have meant that the brand has not kept to the same standard. They must at least keep to the same standard that the customer has been used to. Of course they can improve their offering by giving you a free shoehorn with your shoe purchase. The important point here is, that once they have given an extra shoehorn, they must continue to provide that shoehorn on each and every purchase of a shoe from their brand.

A side lesson to be learned here is that if you improve your offering and you give a better standard to the customer, then that's all very well and lovely but you must stick to this improved offering and new standard otherwise your customer may be unhappy. Many businesses do not understand the importance of keeping standards and just how this affects customers.

First impressions: imagine you are on a blind date and you walk into a restaurant and you don't know who the girl you're going to meet is and in the conversations preceding the meeting you had been talking to a very vivacious, sexy and fiery girl. Upon meeting you see that the girl is dressed like a librarian and looks like your grandmother 50 years ago. Your first impression whether being auditory or seeing a picture was something different and now you're getting another first impression.

You've all heard the saying that you never get a second chance to make a first impression, right? Well, sometimes you do when it comes to a blind date, but that really is an exception to the rule. A first impression is a first impression, and successful businesses spend a lot of time and effort in making sure that that first impression is so amazing and captivating and impressionable that the customer will hopefully be a customer for life.

I remember being on a business class flight with British Airways many years ago and sitting at the front while the flight attendant went through the cabin passing around some hot towels. This particular flight attendant was not keeping with the service that one would expect of a premium cabin on a national carrier; he in fact missed a few people! In a business as big as British Airways, it is probably difficult to keep track of all employees and ensure that they all stick to the same level of standards. However if you are starting a business and you are taking my advice on paying attention to standards, then you will want to be training your staff to be in line with the standards that you have set and the standards that the customer is expecting of your representatives.

So many things make an impression on customers and in a way you have to be very observant and really know your business inside out to make a success of it. For example let's say you're running a hotel, and your rooms are too cold, this could have an effect on whether the guest will come back to that room if it was too cold or too hot. If you are British Airways and your flight attendant didn't give the right food or drink to the customer, this may affect their impression of the overall experience.

Being helpful: this entails a number of things such as recommending other products to people, giving them a great deal of information and being generally helpful. For example, if you have ever shopped in Harrods, you will find that after you've paid for your products, the assistant will usually ask you if you need anything else or help with any directions in store. Such a small thing and something that could easily be adapted by many other stores but it is not. Personally, I have not come across other sales assistants in any other store being as helpful as those in Harrods. This does make an impression and it is one of the many reasons why Harrods is a very well regarded store.

TAXATION

This book does not have the scope to give you comprehensive tax advice. What I would like to point out is that tax is an extremely important part of your business and you must account for it from the very first day. You must be aware of your taxation situation and put aside money for taxes. This includes when you become registered for VAT and more importantly, personal and corporate taxation. Depending on where you live and how good your accountant is, your tax bill can be anything from 0 to 100% of your business! Yes, you read correct. Choosing your accountant is one of the most important business decisions you will ever make, so do not make it hastily.

A good accountant is not your local guy closest to you on the high street. A good accountant is the person that is the accountant of some of the most successful people you know! Even if they cost a little bit more, don't be tight with your money in this area. I have come across so many incapable accountants that have cost their clients so much money that I am so grateful I spent a great deal of time choosing my various accountants.

CONCLUSION

Don't let anyone tell you that doing business is easy and that you are going to start something and immediately be profitable and live happily ever after. If this was the case, everybody would have their own business, be their own boss and have a huge business with lots of profit and no need to work. I have emphasised it many times and will emphasise it again, that all that glitters is not gold. Just because you see someone doing well, it doesn't mean that they are. Just because you have started a business, it doesn't mean that it will become profitable or stay profitable.

Life is a game and the winners are those who understand the rules of the game and stick to the rules and have their eye on winning. Business is a game, in order to be successful you need to stick to the sound rules of the game, not be distracted, not let other competitors throw you out of the game and you must ensure that you are in it to win it, as they say.

I promise you that by sticking to the principles in this book you are going to have a very good chance of having a profitable business with high profits and longevity. The key is to start from the bottom, small, making profits as early as you can and ensuring that you grow slowly, whilst remaining profitable and that you do not lose track of the main objective which is to remain profitable.

I have mentioned this already but will repeat, that whilst many people will give you business advice and pie in the sky theories, what I have been telling you is proven, tried and tested. I have been in business for many years successfully and I'm only giving you the secrets that I have learnt over the last 20+ years of business. Many of the things you have learned in this book, also come from mistakes that I have made and I have pointed them out for you to not make the same mistakes. Any business advisor or mentor, should be a catalyst for you to make more money as quickly as possible. I hope you found this book useful and can use it as a catalyst to start your business and carry on with your business in a profitable way and ensure that you are one of the few that becomes successful in business. The very best of luck to you.

47978009R00065

Printed in Poland
by Amazon Fulfillment
Poland Sp. z o.o., Wrocław